DRC

D1450996

LINE DOGGIE

LINE DOGGIE

Foot Soldier in Vietnam

Charles Gadd

Presidio

To
Sally, David, Laura and Will

CONTENTS

AUTHOR'S NOTE

There have been and will continue to be many books written about Vietnam. Some are historical accounts, some simply state facts and give data, some have tried to distort the truth, and others have attempted to reveal the truth. Many of these writings have painstakingly explained the tactics, war plans, and specific battles, with traces of politics sprinkled in, to try to make the reader understand the Vietnam War.

In the language of guerrilla warfare, there is only one way to describe what the Vietnam conflict was really like, and that is through the eyes of the main character in this dramatic event in American history. Call this individual the "star," "leading actor," "main character," or whatever you wish, but think of him as the "line doggie," a name he was proud to claim. This book is dedicated to all of those who served as infantrymen in Vietnam, especially to those who made the supreme sacrifice.

This is not an authorized history, but merely my story. It is written strictly from memories I have carried for many years and have finally decided to bring forth.

I must explain that this story is written in the first person in order to depict more clearly the horror, fear, joy, and sorrow that practically every line doggie experienced during his tour in one of history's most unpopular wars. Millions of other stories are even more dramatic than those in this book, and every trooper who carried a rifle and rucksack in Vietnam now carries around in his own mind a book full of stories similar to these.

Written some sixteen years after it took place, this story tells how I envisioned the Vietnam War during the late 1960s. I was young and inexperienced and had no doubts that my country was doing the right thing by its involvement in this faraway land. I knew practically nothing about the political relationship between this small country and mine, and merely accepted the fact that "we were right" and "they were wrong" and that was that. Being a product of the post–World War II baby boom, I was brought up hating communism even though I knew very little about it. Serving a year in Vietnam instilled in me the knowledge that communism was truly a reign of horror, and though I still feel our cause was just, I now have doubts and questions that I fear may forever go unanswered.

All of the names in this book have been changed to protect the anonymity of those about whom the stories are written, but all the stories are true—just as I saw them.

CHAPTER ONE

ARRIVAL

It was snowing lightly that morning of December 14, 1967, when our C-141 Starlifter ascended from the runway at Fort Campbell, Kentucky. We were a well-trained group—A Company, 1st Battalion, 501st Infantry—an element of Uncle Sam's proud 101st Airborne Division, the Screaming Eagles. Most of us were replacements from Fort Bragg, North Carolina, belonging to the 82nd Airborne Division and the 18th Airborne Corps. Back in July, our names had come down on a levy from the Department of the Army, which had assigned us to various battalions in the famous 101st. We were originally from every aspect of training that the Army had to offer—military police, armor, artillery, mechanics, clerks, cooks, signal, and many others—but three months of intense infantry training and schooling at Fort Campbell had honed us to the sharpness of expensive cutlery. By December we had trained together in weapons qualification, defensive and offensive tactics and maneuvers, ambush, night movement, and all the other types of training that make an infantry company what it should be. We were proud, gung ho, well trained, and most of all, anxious to leave behind the boredom of garrison duty in the States and find out for ourselves what combat was truly like. A handful of troops from our battalion was returning to Nam for a second tour, and we rookies sensed, through them, that our future was not to be as full of glamour and excitement as we hoped. Little did we know that these men knew what hell was like, for they had been there and back and were about to return.

We pictured ourselves as gallant soldiers going off to war for God, country, and the cause of freedom. None of us could guess that history would record our efforts as being fruitless, and that someday we would confess that "Yeah, I went to Nam, but I'd rather not talk about it!"

We were a small part of a massive airlift of the remaining two brigades of the 101st Airborne Division that had not yet been deployed to Vietnam. The 1st Brigade had been in Nam since 1965, and now the remainder of the division was embarking for "somewhere in Southeast Asia." (It always amused me that our officers were instructed never to admit that we were going to Vietnam. They always used the term "somewhere in Southeast Asia.")

Since we were not traveling by commercial airliner, but by military airlift, we left the States in full combat dress, with helmets, web gear, and rifles stuffed under our seats, and footlockers full of ammunition and grenades strapped to the loading ramp at the rear of the plane. It was not a comfortable flight at all, since the seats had been crammed into this cargo craft and bolted down for the flight. There were no windows, but by some stroke of luck, I happened to sit by a door at the front of the aircraft that had a small circular porthole. During the flight, there seemed to be very little talk—mostly sleeping, reading, and wondering. We stopped first in California for a meal and refueling, then on to that forgotten historic blemish in the vast waters of the Pacific— Wake Island. It amazed me how even the radar at our pilot's fingertips could pick out such a dot in the mighty Pacific. We arrived around midnight and laid over for about two hours for more refueling. Several of us walked down the beaches and stood in awe as we read the monuments to those brave few who had fought so gallantly during World War II for this small, desolate piece of real estate. I walked back into the terminal and bought a postcard to mail to my parents. I had suddenly felt lonely and thought maybe this would break the hollow feeling that welled within me.

The silence on this lonely island was broken by the howl of jet engines as a large plane landed. Some of our group shouted, "Hey, it's a Delta commercial flight. Maybe there are tourists aboard, and we'll get to meet some girls." Everyone nonchalantly walked outside to the "stretch 8." I'm sure most of us were feeling that this would be our last chance for a long time to be seen in uniform before American civilians, and to be able to say, without words, "Yes, we're going to Nam—please be proud of us."

Our feelings of pride and arrogance were suddenly washed away in the warm night air when, to our surprise, about 150 suntanned, khaki-clad GIs off-loaded the airliner and strolled into the terminal. They were Vietnam vets on their way home. Some of them mingled among us and talked quietly. I'm not sure who was more nervous, them or us. It seemed as though they weren't sure whether or not they should be conversing with these so-called "elite troops," and we weren't sure what to say or ask them, since they had been to Nam and we had not.

Our next stop after Wake Island was Manila, where we had breakfast and another hour layover. Every time we got off that airplane, we had a meal, and then were served another meal shortly after taking off again. I remember someone commenting that they were fattening us up for the kill, but those of us who got the joke did not laugh.

Our arrival in Vietnam was around dawn on the morning of December 15th. We landed at Bien Hoa air base, just outside of Saigon, and off-loaded via the tail ramp that was lowered to the apron. Since I had been able to hang on to my treasured porthole seat at the front of the aircraft, I was one of the last to exit. The pilot was a gray-haired, distinguished-looking gentleman, who looked more like a senior senator from South Carolina than an aircraft commander. He had hurried back to the tail ramp to bid us farewell and to say those meaningless little things you say to a total stranger whom you know is going off to participate in real-live war games. Everyone was shaking his hand and saying things like "See you later," "Thanks for the ride," and "Take it easy," but for some reason I felt a need to crack this verbal monotony, so I told him, "Meet me at this same spot, at this same time next year, with this same airplane, and I'll let you take me back home." He smiled, put his hand on my shoulder, and said, "Son, you just keep your ass down and don't try to be a hero for the next 365 days, and I'll be right here waiting on you." I felt as if I had known this man for a long time, and even though I never knew his name, I'll always remember his sincerity. I think he felt he had just delivered us to some unknown fate, and he might be able to ease our nervousness by shaking our hand or telling us "So long." I admired him for this, for he could have taken the easy way out by simply staying in the cockpit until we were gone. Instead, he chose to play the double role of saying good-bye, and at the same time welcoming us to the far-off land of "Charlie Cong."

We boarded several of those olive-drab army buses that sounded just like all the army buses back in the States. It seemed as though some prank-loving mechanic on the assembly line had welded a toy whistle inside the exhaust system so that when the engine accelerated, there was always a distinct whistling sound.

My very first impression of Vietnam was a strange and sickening odor I had never before smelled. Someone asked the bus driver what that awful smell was, and after laughing out loud, he boomed back over the whistling bus engine, "Don't worry, you'll get used to that. It's just Willie, the shit burner." We all laughed as though this simple answer cleared all doubt from our minds, but my friend Bud Dykes leaned over and said, "Who in the hell is Willie the shit burner?" After riding through what seemed to be miles of Quonset huts and tents, we concluded that what Willie did was exactly what his name implied. Willie, as he was always called, was the local Vietnamese senior citizen, usually too old to serve in the military, who was hired by the GIs to dispose of human excrement. All of the base camps had latrines constructed of plywood and screen with a boxed-in bench on the inside, and ten-inch-wide holes sawed in the bench. On the outside rear of these outhouses was a hinged door for placing or removing a sawed-in-two steel drum. These drums served as the receptacles for the latrines and consequently had to be cleaned out daily. This is where Willie came into the picture. The poor old fellow who was unlucky enough to get this job assignment had to open up the back door, slide out the drum, and pour in kerosene, while stirring with a steel fence stake. It usually took about half a day to burn out these barrels, and you could count on finding ol' Willie stooped over a cluster of billowing barrels, always smiling and stirring.

Our bus ride ended at a group of newly constructed buildings that appeared to have been built especially for us, for someone had hung up a banner that read, "Welcome, you bastards of Bastogne." It seemed ironic that we were not associated with the current, unpopular war, but rather with past history and a much more popular conflict.

We spent the rest of the day there and took care of menial chores, such as exchanging our greenbacks for MPCs (military payment certificates), which looked like multicolored play money. I never did figure out who those women were who appeared on the faces of those funny-looking bills. Someone figured they must be the mistresses of all the presidents who appeared on real U.S. currency.

Our first night in Nam was one we would laugh about for some time. Each platoon was assigned to a building for sleeping quarters. The only thing between the four walls of those buildings was a concrete floor, so each man picked out his own little three- by eight-foot section and staked out a claim. Little did we know that the concrete floor would feel like a feather bed compared to some of the other places where we would soon sleep. Sometime after midnight, we were suddenly awakened by a horrendous explosion that sent us all scrambling and flopping about on the floor like a bucket full of freshly caught fish spilled on the deck of a boat. In the total darkness it was every man for himself as we scrambled to find our weapons and helmets, knowing for sure that the gigantic base camp had been overrun and we would soon be involved in hand-to-hand combat. Then one of our old-time returnees laughed and assured us that it was nothing more than an outgoing artillery round and not to worry. The next morning, with a little bit of recon, we found a 175mm fieldpiece less than 100 yards away. This had been the culprit that had scared us to death as it belched out a round directly over our sleeping quarters. Most of us were embarrassed to realize just how green we really were.

We were told we would be departing our new home around noon and to shower and shave while we still had a chance. This area, about the size of a small city block, had one building with running-cold-water showers and even real porcelain toilets instead of the wooden-bench type. After shaving and showering, I realized that Mother Nature was calling. I was surprised she had waited so long, since we had eaten at least seven or eight full meals within the last thirty-six hours. I strolled in among six or eight stalls and carefully picked out a toilet that would honor me. The stalls were nothing more than partitions, without doors, but would adequately serve the purpose. I had been sitting there for two or three minutes, reading a week-old *Stars and Stripes,* when I noticed some weathered feet shuffling around in the stall next to mine. They wore dilapidated sandals, and faded silk pants hung loosely to the ankles. Whoever was attached to those feet was sweeping out the stalls with an old broom worn at a slant into the shape of a triangle. I didn't think much about it and continued my reading, not knowing I was about to learn another custom in this strange land. Those feet were shuffled by an old Vietnamese woman with black teeth (betel nut–stained) who proceeded into my stall and swept around the john as I sat there. I was shocked beyond recovery, but acted as though I had been in this situation many times before. She said *"Chao-ong,"* which I later found out meant "Hello, sir," and upon finishing her sweeping, moved on to the next stall. Not knowing what she had said, I tried to be polite and said, "Yes Ma'am," and she turned around and grinned at me with her ebony teeth. When she moved on, I was up and out of there in less than ten seconds. I don't think I could remember a thing I had read in that *Stars and Stripes.* I would later discover that Vietnam was a country without many toilets, and practically everyone defecated by swinging their buttocks over the edge of a rice dike, or squatting down behind an imaginary tree.

We departed the Bien Hoa base camp as scheduled and boarded two-and-a-half-ton utility trucks (referred to as deuce and a halfs) that were open in the back, like low-sided dump trucks. We sat upon the wooden benches inside the truck beds or stood and held onto the shoulders of our buddies who were perched along the sides. We were told that we were going to a base camp near Cu Chi and our trip would take us through downtown Saigon. This turned out to be the most interesting truck ride of my life. The unknown world of Vietnam, which we had known only through television cameras, finally opened up to us in full splendor. It was hard to realize that this beautiful, bustling city was the nucleus of a war-ravaged country. Beautiful, young women in brightly colored silk dresses and carrying parasols strolled along the sidewalks or rode sidesaddle on the backs of their boyfriends' mopeds. Lambrettas darted through traffic and old buses rolled past us, with a countless number of passengers stuffed within and many more hanging from the sides, standing on narrow running boards. Young children ran alongside our trucks and shouted "Hey GI—You number one—You gimme chop chop—OK?" Several of us made a game out of throwing them cigarettes or sticks of gum, laughing as fifteen or twenty of them converged on the small tidbit and fought over it until one of them emerged victoriously from the pile with the prize clutched tightly in his dirty little fist. The beauty and excitement of downtown Saigon changed as the slums and poorer sections came into view. The houses were jammed up against each other and raw sewage flowed in the gutters. The most interesting thing to me was how the people would take empty beer and Coke cans, cut out the ends, and roll the cans out flat to serve as aluminum shingles for their rooftops.

We were soon riding through the countryside and trying to play the role by looking alert and deadly. Little did we know that the other GIs we passed on the roads, and even the civilians themselves, could immediately tell we were rookies, all the way from our highly polished jungle boots up to the unfaded camouflage covers so tightly fitted upon our helmets. The biggest giveaway was our pale skin; none of us had a bit of suntan, having just come from the cold, gray, December skies of Kentucky.

Since practically none of us knew what a VC was supposed to look like, we assumed anyone in black pajamas was fair game. I remember laughing at Joe Beckley, from New York, when he raised his rifle at an old man walking down the road wearing a faded pair of black pants and shirt. We persuaded Joe that surely other civilians besides the VC wore black clothes. Joe mumbled something and snapped the safety back on his M16. I'm sure if that old papasan knew how close his card had come to being punched, he would have immediately gone home and changed clothes.

CHAPTER TWO

CU CHI

The base camp at Cu Chi was the home of the Wolf Hounds of the 25th Infantry Division, crack troops whose area of operation extended from the outskirts of Saigon westward to the Cambodian border. They had built this sprawling base camp over the past year and now had to relinquish a sector of it to the 2nd Brigade of the 101st. Of course, we acquired the most-run-down sector of the camp and would have to spend the next two or three weeks rebuilding bunkers and sleeping hootches. Our initial assignment was to rebuild our quarters and pull short reconnaissance patrols near the base camp in order to become "climatized," as our leaders called it. We had just come from the midwinter temperatures in Kentucky to the scorching climate of southern Vietnam, and our commanders feared massive heat prostration if we weren't gradually introduced to the hot weather.

We spent the first week at Cu Chi unpacking the Conex boxes that had preceded us there. These large, steel containers had been meticulously loaded back at Fort Campbell with office records and equipment for our administrative personnel, cooking gear for our mess tents, field radios, cots, mosquito nets, crew-served weapons, tools, and every item imaginable to get an infantry company ready for combat within a matter of days. We knew we would be pulling patrols within ten or twelve days, so we labored continually that first week to get ready for the first true test of skills—our first mission. Each of us must have cleaned his personal weapon at least twice a day and yet had not left the confines of base camp to fire off a single round. Sandbags were filled, bunkers re-constructed, showers built, latrines cleaned out, a mess hall set up in an existing building, and platoon-size huts rescreened and cleaned for our sleeping quarters. Our huts were nothing more than plywood floors with screen walls and aluminum siding on the roofs; sandbag walls encompassed the huts to protect us from incoming mortar shells while we slept. Each hut housed two squads, one per side. Mosquito nets hung from the rafters over each cot, and beneath was a wooden ammo box used as a footlocker. We were proud of our little community and had begun to feel at home here, but a major event in the Vietnam War would soon take us away from this "luxury" forever.

For the first few weeks, we got up before dawn and jogged all around the network of dusty roads within the camp. The troops of the 25th made fun of us, for they had never been subjected to rigorous training and discipline such as we knew. We were instructed to stay away from them because of possible fighting, so all we could do to retaliate against their jeering was to call them "legs," a term used by airborne to refer to nonairborne foot soldiers, who had to walk everywhere they went. This seemed to stick in their craw, for deep down inside I believe they were all envious of the famous "Screaming Eagles." There was no love lost between the 25th and the 101st. To show how they felt about us, they gave us "back-row" seats at the Bob Hope Christmas Show when it visited the base camp. We were invited to the show by their com-manders, but were given an arrival time of about five minutes before the show started. Needless to say, we had seats about 100 yards away. I didn't know if I was seeing the real Bob Hope or not; the voice on the PA system sounded like his anyway. I remember writing home and jokingly telling my folks that I got to *hear* Bob Hope in person.

During our second week in Nam, we were all assigned the laborious task of building new bunkers just outside the back door of our hootches. These would not be used for fighting, but for hiding in case we were mortared or rocketed during the night. The bunkers were to be big, holding twenty or so men, so it would take us two or three days of sweat and backaches to dig a big enough hole and fill enough sandbags to finish the job. We started on this project just after breakfast and worked until 4:00 P.M., with everyone from privates to E-6s pitching in to help. On the second day of our bunker construction, an incident occurred I will never forget. We had just started back to work from our lunch break, and everyone was either digging or filling sandbags. The temperature was at least 100 degrees and none of us were ecstatic about our task. Needing to take a break and get a breath of fresh air, I climbed from the hole and walked over to our hootch for a drink of water. Glancing into the hootch, I noticed someone stretched out on a cot, asleep. Since I was an E-5 and a fire-team leader, I felt it necessary to inform whoever was inside that he must come out and work with the rest of us. The shirker turned out to be Terry Hamrickson, a feisty kid from California who couldn't decide if he wanted to be a hippie or a soldier. He had a small frame, but was built like a diesel engine. Since he was so compact, he had volunteered to attend "tunnel-rat" school, which was conducted by the 25th Infantry during the morning hours. His class lasted for a week, and taught how to search and maneuver within the labyrinths of tunnels the VC had built. He had come back from class on this particular day and slipped into the hootch through the front door, without any of us seeing him. Of course he was obligated to work on the bunkers with the rest of us and had no right to sleep the rest of the afternoon.

I went inside and asked Hamrickson what he was doing. His reply was, "Leave me alone, I've just come back from my classes." I told him he did not have the rest of the day off, and to get outside and help us. Then it happened. He jumped up in a craze and started screaming, "Get the hell out of my life!" He then grabbed a hatchet he had purchased back at Fort Campbell. The hatchet was razor sharp, and he had gotten pretty accurate at sticking it into trees or old ammo boxes from about fifty feet away. Grabbing it, he jumped over a cot and swung at my head. I yelped like an old dog with his tail slammed in a screen door as I stumbled backward over cots and ammo boxes. He took another swing at me, and I didn't know whether to block the blows or try to run. I had fears of him throwing it at me if I turned my back to flee from his madness. I must have torn down a half-dozen mosquito nets before he cornered me in the rear of the hootch. He was crying by now and screaming that he was going to cut my face off with his hatchet. I knew then that he was spaced out on drugs, and I instantly decided to make a desperate leap for the opposite wall and lunge through the screen. He was cursing profoundly and drawing his hatchet back for another swing when the door flew open and my friend Bud Dykes shoved a large hunting knife in Terry's face. Bud was a close friend, and we had served in the same MP company at Fort Bragg. He was all soldier and took no lip from anyone. Seeing my predicament, he had decided to get involved and figured there was only one way to get the upper hand. He held his knife up to Hamrickson's neck and called his bluff. Hamrickson broke down and fell to the floor sobbing. I looked at Bud, he looked at me, and neither of us uttered a word; we later admitted to each other that we had never before been so scared. We soon discovered that Hamrickson had made friends with a couple of "pot heads" at tunnel-rat school, and they had taken dope and smoked marijuana after leaving class. He received an Article 15 over the incident and had to relinquish his hatchet to the CO. Believe it or not, we became good friends after that, and would soon find ourselves fighting side by side.

That same night brought even more excitement when we were mortared by enemy gunners from a nearby rubber plantation. The first rounds slammed into our camp area at about midnight, and sent us scrambling out the back door to our half-built bunkers. The only injuries were suffered by those who were first to leap into the topless bunker. They became the landing pad for two squads of GIs clad only in skivvies, as we hurled ourselves into the mouth of that gaping, dark hole. It turned into a riot as those on the bottom cursed loudly when knees, feet, and elbows from unidentified buddies pummeled them unmercifully in the dark. We stood in the hole for two or three minutes as round after round of 80mm mortars whined over our heads through the starlit sky. Someone asked where Bill Rollins was, and after taking a quick head count, we realized he must still be sleeping inside the hootch. Two of us scrambled out of the hole and ran back inside as another mortar round punched through the roof of a nearby supply building and exploded inside. Stubbing toes and scraping shins in the disarranged hootch, we finally found Bill, sleeping like a baby, in his mosquito net–draped cot. How he slept through that melee, I'll never know. We yelled, "Mortar attack!" in his face and brought him to his senses; he was soon charging out the back door with the two of us. Our excitement climaxed as we cheered on the gunships that scrambled from nearby chopper pads. I didn't know whether the pilots were trying to get them airborne to save them from being hit, or whether they were flying off looking for mortar tube flashes. It must have been the latter, for within two or three minutes, we heard miniguns and rockets being fired from the circling choppers into the tree lines. The mortars soon stopped, and we climbed from our bunkers and went back to try to get more sleep.

Dawn came early with the fast-spreading rumor that we were scheduled to go out on our first mission. It was to be a battalion-size operation, with each company sweeping a certain area of the nearby jungle and rendezvousing at dusk to set up a defensive perimeter. Our 81mm mortar teams were to be flown out to the perimeter site, in order to provide us with illumination and HE rounds. This rumor turned out to be true, as the officers called the squad leaders and fire-team leaders to their hootches for a briefing session. This was it!

Our first operation was to be in the famous Hobo Woods, a vast expanse of jungle between Cu Chi and the Cambodian border. It was a VC-infested area so thick with primary and secondary plant growth that it easily snared tanks and APCs as they strained to cut paths through the mass of vines and jungle growth. Our operation started early; we left the rear gate of the base camp just after breakfast and walked at least a mile down a dust-covered road. Engineers cleared our path with mine detectors, and we slowly moved closer to the steaming jungle, which beckoned us like a haunted house at a county fair. We knew this place would be full of evil and wicked things, but our wariness was banished by our desire to explore the unknown. The unmerciful Vietnamese sun climbed quickly and soon demanded that we slow our pace and take a water break every hour or so. I'm sure those men carrying M60 machine guns, or radios, suffered greatly, for even the light load of a rifle and standard field gear was a burden in the nauseating heat. We would later find out that this operation was planned merely to test us in the terrific heat and find out whether we were ready for tougher assignments. Headquarters had picked this sector of Hobo Woods on the advice of the 25th Infantry commanders, since it supposedly was relatively secure and free of VC. This turned out to be a joke, for by noon, Charlie Company of our Geronimo Battalion had run into stiff resistance from a small element of highly evasive VC. They struck fast and hard, quickly killing two of our rookie troops and wounding three others. We could hear the firefight in the distance and cautiously moved on, not knowing what was happening or what might happen to us.

As we left the road, our pace slowed to about ten feet every five minutes. I had never been in such thick undergrowth, even in my boyhood days of following a pack of rabbit dogs through the North Carolina woods. We soon found out, first hand, what a "wait-a-minute bush" was. We had heard about this from other vets, and now knew what it was that every line doggie in Vietnam had learned to curse in his sleep.

This humorous name was given out of respect to a small, treelike bush that crouched among the jungle growth and lashed out at its victims with the ferocity of a rabid badger. Its long, spindly branches were covered with thorns resembling straightened-out fish hooks, which would go right through our clothing and embed their needlelike heads in our flesh. The name for this "carnivorous" plant must have originated when the very first GI who encountered it had to quietly beckon his buddies moving ahead to "Wait a minute!" Everyone would have to stop as the victim carefully unwrapped himself from the clutches of this pesky plant. This bush seemed to have an evil heart, for it usually caught its victim in such tender places as the neck, behind the ear, in the armpit, and worst of all, in the crotch.

We hacked our way forward with machetes, while keeping a reading on our compasses. There were no landmarks to guide us, so we constantly had to keep track of our paces and shoot an azimuth as we studied our maps to see where we were supposedly heading. Without warning, the thick undergrowth would spit us out into a clearing, which was usually dotted with tunnel openings and bunkers. We knew these tunnels might be holding a squad of VC, quietly and patiently waiting to spray us with AK rounds. The VC would then disappear into the network of underground avenues only to come up 100 yards away and easily escape into the jungle without us ever laying an eye on them. We grew very tense from not being able to see more than ten feet in front of us. The sweat that drenched our fatigues became cold and clammy as the tension blended with the misery of the heat.

We hacked through the jungle for the entire day, finally cutting our way out into a large field covered with scrub brush and sunbaked grass, which stretched for at least a quarter of a mile. This was our rendezvous point. The entire battalion had already assembled and started setting up a large, circular perimeter, with each company manning a crescent-shaped sector. Our company was the last to move into position. The CO gave orders to our platoon leaders, showing them where to locate our defensive positions for the night. It was a relief to be out of that jungle even to be digging a foxhole. Each position was assigned three men, and we were told we would get a box of C rats as soon as our foxholes were dug. The soil was soft and sandy, so the holes were soon completed. As dusk approached, we sat on the edge or stood in our foxholes and slowly savored our first meal since breakfast. I can well remember how good that can of cold ham and eggs tasted as I washed it down with warm, iodine-flavored water from my canteen.

Fields of fire were determined for each position, claymore mines set out, and hand grenades removed from our web gear and pressed into the soft earth piled in front of our foxholes. We felt security and power as darkness approached, for what idiot would attack a battalion of U.S. army paratroopers? Our 81mm mortars were prepared and ready for supporting our perimeter. Each company had its own heavy weapons platoon positioned just behind its sector; the main mission was H and I (harassing and interdictory) firing throughout the night. Here we were. Some of the best Uncle Sam had to offer, ready to meet head-on with the best Uncle Ho had to offer. I felt proud as I sat on the edge of our foxhole and started the first watch with Bud and Roger Clapeckni stretched out on the grass behind me trying to sleep.

I felt a need to double-check my readiness, so I reached out in the dark and reassured myself as to where each grenade and each claymore detonator lay on the mound of earth before me. I reached up to give a tug at my steel pot and touched the squeeze bottle of mosquito lotion held tightly beneath the elastic band around my helmet. This reminded me that I had not yet taken precautions against the millions of mosquitoes that had just begun to visit each foxhole in search of any square inch of flesh not covered with clothing or mosquito lotion. This lotion was a strong-smelling concoction, oily in texture and tasting like diesel fuel. Because of its taste, most of us rarely spread it on our lips; so it wasn't unusual for us to rouse at dawn with lips swollen from at least a dozen mosquito bites. Mosquitoes were a constant menace to us at night, and I never got used to them buzzing in my ears or flying nonchalantly into my open mouth. Once, in disgust, I tried to imagine how many times the GIs in Vietnam had been bitten by mosquitoes and just how much American blood had been sucked out by these insects instead of spilled in combat. My conclusion was that these damned pests had drunk enough of our body fluids to bloody the Mississippi River from New Orleans to St. Louis.

About 3:00 A.M. I was pulling my third watch of one hour on and two hours off. I sat on the edge of the foxhole listening to our mortar teams preparing to fire more H and I rounds over our heads and into the sleeping jungle. I found it interesting to listen to them bark out their orders for a fire mission. Each command was crisp and precise as the fire controller verbally led his men through their paces in total darkness. I pictured their actions in my mind as someone hollered, "Hang fire!" A second later came the command, "Fire," as the gunner released the round and sent it backsliding down the tube where it made contact with the firing pin. The round discharged with a solid "whump," which reminded me of a new car door slamming tightly shut. I listened to each shell being fired, as the gunners barked out their jargon. The acoustics of the thick, dark jungle quickly swallowed up the explosions as the rounds arched over our heads and found their targets. The mortar teams continued to fire at a rate of about two rounds every five minutes.

I was about to climb from the hole and wake up Bud for his watch when tragedy struck. A round was fired, and I instantly knew something was different. Instead of the explosive ring from the steel mortar tube, there was a pop and a loud buzz. Not recognizing the sound, I froze, awaiting some kind of explanation of this strange noise. Then to my immediate right there was a blinding flash, and a jolting shock wave raced by my body and sped away. My first reaction was to reach out and grab my buddies, since I thought we were being attacked. Dragging them into the hole with me, I could hear someone screaming for help. There was no ensuing firefight, which puzzled me; only the screams of wounded soldiers filled the night. I started to crawl toward the screams, only two holes over from my own, but realized that the medics and the CO were already on the scene and I could do nothing. For more than an hour none of us knew what had occurred; finally our platoon leader, Lieutenant Hernandez, crawled over and told us the sickening news. The explosion had come from one of our own mortar rounds. Instead of firing normally, it had misfired and sputtered less than 100 feet from the gun. The dud traveled just far enough to arm itself, and exploded as it landed less than two feet away from one of our positions. A soldier sitting up in the foxhole was decapitated and another was critically injured as he slept less than five feet away. The third suffered only burst eardrums because the GI he slept beside had absorbed the jagged shards of shrapnel.

A medevac chopper soon flew in to evacuate the dead and wounded and then everything was suddenly quiet again. Gloom settled down on us along with the cool, wet dew and none of us slept for the remainder of the night. I remember hearing the CO's voice as he called up battalion headquarters and gave a "sit-rep" (situation report). His words brought a chill to my heart—"One KIA—two WIA." The thought of our own guns doing this wasteful thing was unbearable. And this kind of tragedy would occur again—not once, but several times.

When morning came, we moped around and privately mourned our friends. No one said much, but everyone's feelings could be seen in his expression. We later learned that the faulty mortar ammunition had been drawn from an ammo dump of the 25th Division. This particular ammo was traced to records showing damage by moisture—it was listed to be destroyed. By someone's careless mistake, the ammo was issued to us and A Company's first casualties resulted. We were all angry about this senseless error, as we tried to cope for the first time with the death of a friend and a fellow soldier.

We stayed in the Hobo Woods for two more days and made no contact. Without realizing it, we were learning fast. We were beginning to function like the freshly oiled parts of a well-tuned engine, and with major events soon to happen, we would need all the experience we could get. We returned to base camp, where we were greeted with cold showers, iced-down beer, and thin, but juicy steaks.

We spent the next two days at camp, during which time we were assigned a South Vietnamese soldier to play the dual role of scout and interpreter. His name was Tan Lo. He was overly friendly, had a bucktoothed smile, and was as skinny as a six-foot-long piece of dental floss. He spoke fluent English and several of us asked him to teach us certain phrases in Vietnamese. He would soon prove valuable as an interpreter. By some act of fate, I was dubbed with the same title, since I could speak French fairly well. I had no idea that my two years of high-school French and two years of college French would serve me in such a strange way. It turned out that many South Vietnamese had learned the language during the French occupation of the fifties. I had never made decent grades in my French classes and on top of that, I spoke the language with a North Carolina accent, but none of the Vietnamese spoke French very well either, so ironically, we understood each other.

After two days at base camp, we went on another operation. This one led us out the opposite side of the camp into a countryside covered with large rice paddies, rubber plantations, and small villages. This operation was more enjoyable, as we made sweeps through the villages and got to see the peasants and how they lived. A lesson we learned quickly was that when the women and children moved about the villages in a normal fashion, there was not much to worry about. When the North Vietnamese or Viet Cong were around, the natives would leave the area, for to them, the presence of North Vietnamese and an element of U.S. soldiers close by was a sure recipe for trouble and destruction. Moving through a deserted village always made us nervous and trigger happy.

Having swept through a small village, we started across a large rice field. It had recently been harvested, so the walking was easy. We had gone about halfway across when suddenly a sniper started taking well-aimed shots at us from the far side. Everyone scrambled for the cover of the two-foot-high dikes that crisscrossed the paddy. Looking for as much cover as possible, I noticed what appeared to be a foxhole dug right in the middle of the dike, and without giving it a second thought, I jumped in feet first. What I had hoped was a foxhole turned out to be an irrigation well about twenty feet deep. My first thought was that this must be an express lane to hell, for it seemed as though I plunged downward for ten minutes. The well was almost dry, and when I reached the bottom, I drove my feet into about four feet of puddinglike mud. I wasn't worried about being rescued, for my first glance upward caught the puzzled faces of two buddies. Realizing my predicament, they broke into laughter, and I could hear one of them call for a rope between outbursts of uncontrollable guffaws. It took six men to pull me out of that slimy ooze, and I too joined in the laughter when I stood up and looked down at the mess that covered me from head to foot. My rifle and equipment were unrecognizable. I reached into my pockets and pulled out a handful of muck with little, soft-bodied creatures swimming around in it. We soon came to a canal that had to be crossed, so while everyone else used a small footbridge, I chose to wade, and consequently held up the entire column for ten minutes while I took a bath with all my clothes and equipment on.

Later that afternoon, we discovered some coconut palms laden with fruit. A couple of well-aimed rounds from an M16 brought down a cluster of five or six coconuts, and we hacked at them with machetes to get at the treat inside the leathery husks. We drank the cool, sweet milk and then divided the moist chunks of coconut meat. It was delicious and filling, but those of us who partook soon suffered from our gluttony. In less than two hours, we became deathly sick with stomach cramps and the miseries of diarrhea. The medics gave us chalky white tablets which helped some, but our suffering would last through most of that night and into the next day.

The following day we received a radio report from battalion that Bravo Company had a trooper who was missing in action. They discovered him missing the night before when the company formed its defensive perimeter. They had done a lot of canal crossing that day on several makeshift footbridges assembled from rope or downed trees, and their explanation was that he had possibly fallen from one of the bridges and drowned without anyone seeing him. We were instructed to swing over about a mile and search the area where Bravo had been the day before. We found some of their crossing points at various spots on the canals and small rivers, but saw no traces of the missing soldier. We even threw grenades into the deep waters to try to dislodge his body if he were down there at all. The only results we got were hundreds of dead fish that bellied up and floated to the surface. We searched for that lost soldier for most of the day and were about to reassemble for our night perimeter when the word came down that they had found the lost private. As feared, he had fallen into deep water while crossing a canal and was unable to get out of the belts of machine-gun ammo draped around his neck. It was assumed that, with this weight, along with his other gear, he had panicked and gone straight to the bottom. We never found out how they located his body, but at least his was one name that would not remain on the MIA lists.

That evening, our squad was assigned the mission of moving about a mile from our company perimeter and setting up an ambush at a small bridge. We had moved through the same area earlier that day, so we knew where we were going. The only problem would be darkness. Bill Rollins was our squad leader, and Bud and I were fire-team leaders. We assembled our squad and showed them on the map the route we would take. Terry Hamrickson would walk point with a Starlight Scope mounted on his M16. This would enable him to literally see in the dark as he methodically led us from one checkpoint to another. Our ambush patrol started without a hitch. Each of us had stripped from our bulky gear and carried nothing but a weapon, grenades, claymores, and 100 rounds each of machine-gun ammo. We wore "flop hats," since steel pots would stand out under the starlit sky like the glass globe of a streetlight. We darkened our faces and hands with camo grease and stuck small branches of leaves in our hats. Every other man carried a poncho liner to sleep on, stuffed in his shirt, since half of us would be awake at all times. Artillery grids were plotted in advance in case we needed immediate support of HE rounds or illumination.

It took us more than an hour and a half to go halfway, for we were being cautious and sure of every step. This was definitely VC country, and we were on our first night patrol, so no one had the desire to rush into something. I soon realized that my fatigues were drenched with perspiration, which should not have been, since a light breeze stirred the cool night air, blowing away all traces of the day's stifling heat. This cold sweat was a result of the gut-gnawing tension that only a line doggie could experience. I tried to take my mind off the tense atmosphere, but every time I saw Terry suddenly crouch and peer through the Starlight Scope, I feared he had noticed something that would mean trouble.

We finally reached our destination, and "Hud" Bowers and I went ahead to secure the ambush zone. We had practiced this many times back at Fort Campbell and each of us knew exactly what was needed to accomplish our task. We moved forward slowly and split apart to arch out and meet on the opposite side of the site. Together, we came back through the middle and picked out suitable spots to locate our positions. We then crept back about 100 yards to the waiting squad and silently briefed each squad member on the situation. It took us another twenty minutes to move forward and position ourselves near the bridge. The silence was suddenly broken by the faint cry of a baby in the distance, and I cringed to think of an infant so close to this potential danger zone. The crying soon ceased, and we proceeded to set up our ambush.

All positions were in and secure when it came time for Bud Dykes to move into the "kill zone" and set up two trip flares. He had finished with one and was setting up the other when it exploded in his hands, illuminating everything around us with the intensity of a million candles. Some of us froze and others dove for cover, while Bud bravely picked up the spewing chunk of white phosphorus in his bare hands and hurled it into the river. The blinding light was gone as suddenly as it appeared, leaving all of us with absolutely no trace of our night vision. Blindly, I worked my way over to Bud and found him doubled over his still-smoking hands. He was mute with pain, and he later told me that if he had opened his mouth to talk, screams would have come out instead. We had blown our own ambush and quickly decided on a point to withdraw. We fired our claymores, gathered up our gear, and hurried away much more quickly than we had come. The rest of the night was spent huddled in thick undergrowth. With his pain, Bud didn't sleep at all, and the next morning we called in a medevac for him, before returning to the company.

We spent several days on this operation before returning to base camp. Back at camp, knowing we would spend a couple of days there before returning to the fields, we settled down to cleaning weapons and equipment and writing as many letters as possible to loved ones back home. Traces of boredom could be seen around the company area, since most of us wanted to get back to the fields and rice paddies. I can't remember whose suggestion it was, but someone came up with the bright idea of distinguishing ourselves from the 1st and 2nd Platoons by giving each other Mohawk haircuts. We pulled out some old clippers and proceeded to shave our heads except for a two-inch strip from front to back. Three or four heads had been completed, and as I was sitting down for my turn, the first sergeant burst into our hootch, demanding an explanation for this "unsoldierly-like conduct." I really think he was laughing under his breath, but his professionalism told him to correct this deed that was strictly against SOP. He instructed that no more heads would be cut in this fashion, and that everyone with a Mohawk would have their strips shaved off at once. This deflated our egos somewhat, but we knew we would soon come up with another crazy idea that would be just as much fun.

It wasn't long before someone suggested that we construct a sign to hang over the front door of our hootch, to let every passerby know that the "mighty 3rd Platoon" inhabited this humble shack. All kinds of suggestions were hashed over and we finally agreed on one. It would be a sign with a title in bold letters that read "The Mighty Third." Beneath it would be a helmet pulled down tightly over highly polished jungle boots; the helmet would appear to be quivering and shaking as bullets flew all around. This idea originated from the never-ending comical remarks of our platoon sergeant, Eddie Hands. He would often comment in a joking way that when the going got tough, simply pull down your helmet tightly over your boot tops and wait till a lull in the fighting. Then come out from under your helmet and "fight like hell." This was his way of trying to ease tension and calm our nerves whenever we knew that a firefight was inevitable.

In all honesty, the sign was a tribute to Sergeant Hands, since we all felt a deep respect for him. Sergeant Eddie Hands was one of the best platoon sergeants to ever serve in Vietnam. He was truly a professional soldier, who knew every aspect of his trade and who had that uncanny knack of always doing everything by the book while appearing to be doing things his own way. His greatest asset was his ability to lead men. He was always thinking of his troops and constantly put himself last when it came to the safety and well-being of his platoon. I can remember watching him pick up the remains of a case of C rations after it had been picked over for the best meals by hungry soldiers. I don't know how, but he continued to survive on those horrid cans of ham and limas. He was a tall, somewhat thin, black man with smooth skin the color of oiled mahogany and dark brown eyes that gave you a feeling of warmth and comfort. The only time I ever heard him complain was when he felt his troops were not getting a fair shake or were being pushed to the point of exhaustion by some ridiculous order that had come down from battalion. Sergeant Hands was the backbone of our platoon, and in the coming months we would all grow to love and respect him in a strong father-son relationship.

The next day we were wakened around 3:00 A.M. and told to pack only our combat gear for an extended stay away from Cu Chi base camp. There was tension in the air among the officers, and we knew something big was about to happen. We strapped and tied everything we could carry to our rucksacks and waited for further orders. After a quick breakfast, we saddled up and made the long, dusty march to the small airstrip on the far side of the base camp. Here we waited for another two hours and watched as several C-130 Hercules cargo planes flew in and loaded up whole companies of our comrades and flew off into the warm morning sky. Finally our turn came to load one of those fat, camouflaged transports, without yet knowing where we were going. After we had stuffed our gear under the web seats and fastened our seat belts, our CO spoke over the plane's intercom in order to be heard above the whining drone of the idling engines. Everyone strained to hear the explanation we had so patiently waited for. We were about to be introduced to a major event in the history of the Vietnam War—Tet.

CHAPTER THREE

TET

A major offensive, now referred to as the Tet Offensive of 1968, had just been launched by massive elements of VC and NVA, from the Mekong Delta to the DMZ. Whole cities had come under siege, and the allied forces had been struck to their knees after a night-long surge against everything from small fire-support bases to the U.S. Embassy in Saigon. The American commanders reeled to counterattack and immediately started relocating fighting units to crucial weak spots throughout the country. This was where we came in. Our destination was now known to be the I Corps area, which would put us about twenty miles south of the treacherous DMZ.

We wondered if we would ever return to Cu Chi and the small base camp "neighborhood" we had come to enjoy. Little did we know that we would never again see this particular area of South Vietnam—we were destined to travel north and spend the rest of our tour engaging elements of the North Vietnamese as they slipped over the DMZ or entered the country through the northern lanes of the famous Ho Chi Minh Trail.

We landed at the Hue/Phu Bai airport and immediately boarded deuce and a halfs for another unknown destination. Our convoy headed south and soon came to a small group of hills that was bustling with GIs and military vehicles. This was the ground breaking of what would be known as Camp Eagle. We were some of the first troops to build part of this base camp, and we labored for three days building bunkers and stringing concertina wire. We had heard that a large enemy offensive had taken place, but due to the importance of constructing this new base camp, we were being kept away from the major battle areas.

On the morning of our fourth day at Camp Eagle, we again boarded trucks and this time headed north on Highway One. Our journey took us through the deserted streets of Hue, and we were told by the MPs leading our convoy to be alert and ready for anything. We sensed that things were bad as we drove through this large city, for practically no civilians were seen and the air was charged with the sensation of danger. Our convoy snaked its way through the city and continued northward along the potholed surface of Highway One. We rolled through the countryside and saw no sign of life for at least ten miles. I noticed that several small, grass huts had miniature yellow and red flags hung over their doors to show they sided with the South Vietnamese and not the enemy.

We entered the small town of Hai Lang and drove through it as though we were securely within the confines of our old base camp. In less than a week, we would be engaged in vicious combat in this very village. We rode to the far side of Hai Lang and turned onto a one-lane dirt road that ran alongside the local schoolhouse. We thought this was our destination, but we continued on for four or five miles into the foothills of a small mountain chain. The terrain in these rolling hills was devoid of trees and was sparsely covered with grass and scrub brush clustered as though huddled for protection from the roaming armies. Our convoy stopped and we sat puzzled, for there was no sign of civilization, much less a base camp. The narrow dirt road ended abruptly on the side of the hill, so we guessed this must be the place, but we wondered where we were and what we were going to do next. A Huey soon flew in and off-loaded a group of high-ranking officers, who approached our CO. They seemed to be giving him instructions as they stared off in the distance and pointed their rifles in various directions. I remember laughing as I imagined them making some real-estate transaction, purchasing part of this barren stretch of South Vietnam, with us as part of the underhanded deal. When they climbed back into the chopper and flew away, it gave us a lost and lonely feeling.

We were quickly dispersed around a small hill and told to dig in. Again, we dug foxholes and set up defensive positions in which to spend the night. The boredom of digging holes, and then moving to another location to dig more holes, was taking its toll. Our hands were covered with blisters, our backs ached, and our morale was reaching an all-time low. None of us thought of ourselves as base camp soldiers, yet this chore of building new base camps and fire bases seemed to be our only mission in this war. The fire base was named LZ Jane. On our second day, artillery pieces were flown in and tons of equipment arrived to build a small but effective fire base there in the rolling foothills.

War came calling during our second night at LZ Jane. The dark, cloud-covered sky quickly erupted in yellow flashes that were woven into the black night with the erratic flight of red tracers. We were under attack! It was around 3:00 A.M. and I was asleep on the rocky ground just behind our foxhole. A sudden barrage of explosions and machine-gun bursts erased the silence of night. The attack had come on the opposite side of the perimeter from us, but we were receiving stray mortar shells and hundreds of stray machine-gun and rifle rounds. An artificial dawn erupted as artillery and mortar teams rushed to their guns and fired round after round of illumination shells. The pale yellow light from the illumination gave the landscape an eerie glow that would enable us to detect enemy movement among the scattered brush and rolling hills.

Our positions were poised and ready, but the enemy never showed himself on our sector of the perimeter. The main attack was some 200 yards away, and these troopers were catching hell. An element of about fifty North Vietnamese had crawled, undetected, beneath the single coil of concertina wire that had been strung the day before. They attacked with RPG rocket launchers, 80mm mortars, automatic rifles, and satchel charges. A suicide squad armed with only satchel charges was assigned the job of charging the bunkers and foxholes and slinging their packages of explosives into the positions of fighting GIs. Several bunkers were blown apart, leaving smoldering piles of sandbags and dismembered bodies. The destroyed positions left gaping holes in the defensive perimeter, and several NVA raced through and headed for the TOC (tactical operations center), located at the middle of the fire base. They were met by gun-wielding cooks and clerks, who cut them down as they raced by their tents. The melee continued for several minutes and in the confusion, no one was safe within the perimeter, since heavy fighting was taking place inside as well as outside the bunker line. We later heard that a mechanic had tackled an NVA soldier and stabbed him to death with a screwdriver. This was truly hand-to-hand fighting, and many stories of valor would come out of the attack against LZ Jane.

The enemy had been quick, effective, and deadly. Morning brought the grim task of counting the dead. The final count was thirty-five dead NVA and thirteen dead GIs. That day we spent several hours stringing more wire and setting out dozens of claymore mines and trip flares. Cases of grenades and rifle ammunition were distributed to each position in case of another attack on our small fire base. A track-mounted "duster" outfitted with twin 40mm cannons was brought in and positioned in the middle of our platoon's sector, and we soon got to know the tank crew pretty well. They seemed to be a carefree bunch, who relied on their massive fighting machine to protect them from whatever might come along. I felt they were a different breed of soldier from us— their hair was shabby and dirty; most of them wore a stubby beard; and they were always covered with a pasty coating of grease, dirt, dust, and sweat. Yet, they won our respect and friendship with their gutsy spirit and jovial attitude. I learned that living, eating, and sleeping on an armored vehicle allowed little time or opportunity for personal hygiene, and it wouldn't be long before we too would look the same from living in the jungles of Vietnam.

The next day orders came for Lieutenant Hernandez to take one squad and move to the outskirts of Hai Lang. Our squad was picked and the duster assigned to go with us, so we all climbed on and headed back down the dusty road toward the small village. Having never ridden on a track vehicle before, several of us climbed on the back, which proved to be a serious mistake. The exhaust vent belched out hot diesel fumes, and by the time we arrived at our destination, we were nauseated from the exhaust and practically cooked from the intense heat.

As we approached the schoolhouse on the outskirts of Hai Lang, we saw several dead NVA soldiers lying in the sand. They obviously had been killed by the ARVN soldiers who manned a small camp directly across Highway One from the schoolhouse. We moved into the ARVN camp and talked with their two Green Beret advisors, who told us that the NVA had attacked their camp the same night LZ Jane was attacked. A battalion of NVA soldiers had moved into Hai Lang and was there to stay. They advised us not to enter the village with such a small force. One of our troops climbed on top of an ARVN bunker to get a better look into the village, and a well-aimed bullet blew the stock off of his M16.

We stayed in the ARVN camp for most of the day and rode the duster back to LZ Jane before dusk. Four of us scrambled to be the first ones aboard so we could sit as far away from the exhaust vent as possible. The tank commander laughed at us, not saying a word. I was sure he knew why we wanted a front seat and I cursed him under my breath. He had allowed us to cling to the exhaust grate on the trip into Hai Lang, knowing full well that we would roast our buns.

The next morning brought orders for us to saddle up: this time our whole company was going back to Hai Lang. We walked the dirt road, wondering what lay ahead in this small village. Reaching the schoolhouse at midday, we came upon the remains of Delta Company, which had moved into the village earlier that morning. They were practically annihilated. They had managed to bring out the wounded, for evacuation, but had to leave several bodies in the middle of the town. Bud and I recognized an MP buddy from Fort Bragg and asked him what had happened. "If you don't have to go in there, then don't go!" he told us. "I'm the only one left out of my entire squad." His comment didn't help our nervousness any, for we had just received word that we would soon be going into the village, and the "Mighty Third" would lead the way.

Our squad was given point, and we were instructed to move into the village to a crossroad and hold up there. We spread out and took our time moving from one grass hootch to another—with rifles held at ready, the safeties switched on automatic. We kept our voice commands at a minimum, using hand signals where possible, and moved slowly forward, searching out every hedgerow, animal pen, haystack, and hootch. Bud scared us to death when he stepped inside a hootch and fired point-blank at his own image in a large mirror. We moved on past three or four more houses, and then the whole world exploded around us. We had walked into an ambush. Mortar rounds started splashing all around, while machine-gun bullets cut down the hedges of bamboo that we leaped behind. RPG rockets buzzing over our heads tore off tree limbs and rooftops. We were caught up in fire so intense that no one had yet figured out which direction it was coming from.

When the ambush was sprung, I was walking past the front of a cinder-block hootch with a grass roof. The front wall was open, with a two-foot-wide cinder-block pillar supporting the roof at the center of the opening. I lunged behind the pillar. Machine-gun bullets tore off chunks of concrete from the blocks and sent them stinging into my face and neck. Each time I tried to peer out, bullets tore off more of the edges, and I would quickly straighten up to catch my breath and wait for a lull. But there was no lull. The firing was getting heavier and more effective as the enemy gunners lowered their field of fire to about knee level. Someone was shouting for a medic, but there was no way Doc Reems could get to us.

I managed to catch a glimpse of Bud as he crawled like a lizard from a clump of bamboo that was getting shorter and shorter, as though it were being mowed by a giant, invisible lawn mower. He slithered over to a small depression in the yard and lay there, trying to get a bearing on the origin of the fire. He saw me crouched behind the pillar and yelled for me to try to fire into the hootch about seventy feet in front of us. He thought he had seen gunfire coming from under the straw roof. I stood up, stepped out from behind my hiding place, and emptied a magazine into the hootch. Before I could jump back to my shelter, something hit me in the stomach with the force of a line drive. It knocked the breath out of me and rolled me across the hard earthen floor. Still conscious, I was afraid to look at my stomach, afraid of seeing entrails hanging over my belt. I reached down, certain I would put my hands in a pool of warm, wet blood, but found nothing. I rolled to my knees, still choking for breath, and managed to climb back to my hiding place. I heard another call for a medic and looked out to see Lieutenant Hernandez trying to drag the body of Roy Kleiner back to safety. I knew instantly that Roy was dead, because his eyes were open and had rolled back in his head. There was a small, blood-stained hole in his shirt, right over his heart. The telltale sign of no bleeding told me his heart had stopped. At that moment a rocket tore half the roof off my hootch; the bamboo rafters fell and knocked me to my knees. It was then that I noticed Joe Maldonado crawling out from under the rubble and crossing himself while repeating "Hail Mary." This sight struck me as humorous and I laughed out loud. Joe was not amused, however, and screamed, "What in the hell are you laughing at?"

More rockets, mortar rounds, and tracers poured in on us. Finally the loud "whop, whop, whop" of a low-flying gunship could be heard over the din. It was one of our Cobras laying down a barrage of rocket and minigun fire. Everything suddenly seemed brighter, until another gunship appeared and mistakenly fired rockets at *us* instead of the NVA. The hootch that I had fired at disappeared in a clap of thunder and a bright orange fireball. Flaming chunks of thatched roof rained down on us, adding to our fear and confusion. Several of us were now returning fire in the general direction of the incoming rounds, but we still had no definite targets. Another call for a medic turned my head to see Roger Clapeckni holding his hand with a bullet hole punched neatly through the fleshy base of his thumb. Bill Rollins raced over to tie off his bleeding hand and was hit squarely in the butt with a tracer round. It spun him around and knocked him face first into a small vegetable garden in the yard. He yelled, "I'm hit!" and I left my position to help drag him back. Dark liquid quickly stained the seat of his pants, and I pulled out my knife to cut off his pant leg. It was then I realized that the liquid was grape Kool-Aid. Bill had been hit in his canteen. The bullet had hit the container squarely in the center, and the impact made Bill think he had been shot. The slug had pierced his canteen cup, then his plastic canteen, and stopped as it reached the sweet liquid contents. Bill pulled out his canteen and grinned from ear to ear as he rattled the bullet around inside.

"Fast Herm" Hope from Miami crawled over to me and shouted that we were withdrawing. I glanced around and saw three or four soldiers low-crawling and trying at the same time to drag the body of Roy Kleiner. Heavy machine-gun fire was still coming in, so Sgt. Tom Moore and I stayed to return as much fire as possible. As we fired our M16s, I noticed my ammo was almost expended. So when Tom yelled that we were the only two left and it was time to move back with the rest of the company, I totally agreed with him. Together we crawled on our stomachs for at least 100 yards.

When we finally reached the rest of the company, we realized we had been separated from our platoon. They had withdrawn to the schoolhouse. I then heard Bud's voice asking if anyone had seen me. He thought I had been hit, and he was going back to the village to find me. His dirty face looked good to me as he threw his arm around my shoulder and solemnly asked if I knew about our casualties. We trudged back to the schoolhouse to join the rest of the platoon and walked over to Roy's body, which was wrapped in his own poncho. We knelt beside the corpse to pay our last respects, and a lump rose in my throat as I tried to speak. Without a word, Bud and I quietly rose and just walked away.

Darkness would soon be upon us, so we formed a company perimeter around the schoolhouse and dug in for the night. The village was being hammered with artillery shells from LZ Jane, and some of the rounds were landing so close to us that shrapnel hit two of our troops before we could get dug in. Night came, and so did the rain. An initial downpour soaked us to the bone; then it settled down to a slow, steady drizzle. The land at this end of the village was pure-white sand, so digging our foxholes was easy. But when the rain started, the sand stuck to us like glue, and the holes began to cave in. I shared a position with Hud Bowers and Sergeant Hands, and halfway through the night, Hud and I had to dig out Sergeant Hands from under a cave-in. As he had slept curled up in one corner of our foxhole, three feet of wet sand had slid down over him.

The artillery barrage continued throughout the night. Some rounds were landing extremely close, and I heard Lieutenant Hernandez call our FO on the radio and ask him for an adjustment in the firing. Before this could be done, a large shell screamed over our heads and slammed into a building across the road from us. The building was adjacent to the small ARVN compound and was serving as sleeping quarters for the families of the Vietnamese soldiers. It was full of women and children, and their screams could be heard over the continuing explosions of the artillery shells. We had not even known they were in the building, since the ARVN soldiers had just moved their families there in order to protect them from the North Vietnamese. We watched under the shadowy light of the illumination shells as the Vietnamese soldiers tried to rescue their loved ones from the smoldering rubble. I felt helpless and extremely depressed as I watched them carry the dead and wounded back to the compound.

It was a long, sleepless night, and the discomfort of the wet sand and cold rain added to our misery. The day had been filled with death and destruction and now the night had become equally horrible. Dawn brought light to a dirty, gray sky that continued to shower us with a cold, steady rain. The sky seemed to reflect our mood as we were told we would be returning to the village. No one was overly anxious to go back in, but we all wanted a chance to strike back at the enemy that had kicked our tails the day before.

Before leaving, we were given a chance to eat some C's and boil ourselves a cup of coffee in our canteen cups. Most of us had used up all of our heating tablets, so Bill broke open a claymore mine and cut the plastic explosive into small chunks. This material burned like fury and made excellent fuel for heating C rats and coffee. The hot coffee felt good as it took away some of the chill from spending the night in wet fatigues. We also used this time to brush some of the menacing sand from our clothes and equipment. Most of our rifles were choked with the white grit and would require cleaning before going back into Hai Lang. My ammo pouches, fastened to the front of my pistol belt, were full of sand. This had happened when I had crawled out of the village on my stomach. Each pouch held magazines of M16 cartridges, and I had used up all the pouches but one. I set about refilling the empty magazines and cleaning the ones I had not fired. This required removing the rounds of ammo, wiping them off, and then refilling the magazines. It was then that I discovered something that made my blood run cold.

When I opened the ammo pouch to remove the unspent magazines, I noticed a large tear in the front of the heavy canvas pouch. I removed the magazines and was shocked to find two of them distorted beyond recognition. The cartridges inside were bent double into the shape of horseshoes. These full magazines had evidently deflected a large-caliber machine-gun bullet that was destined to tear through my lower abdomen. All the puzzle pieces suddenly fell together and I remembered being pelted in the stomach and having the breath knocked out of me. In the excitement of the firefight, I had quickly forgotten about the incident. I made a point to show Bill these souvenirs, since he had made a big issue out of his canteen. Everyone was amazed at how the magazines and bullets had been smashed into twisted metal, and yet I did not have a scratch. I wrapped the ammo and magazines in an old rag and stuffed them into my rucksack as a good-luck piece. I hoped to be able to carry them home, but as chance would have it, I would soon lose them in another heated firefight.

We saddled up and began our gut-grinding trek back into Hai Lang. We went in with each platoon spread out in a side-by-side formation. This would prevent us from being hit from two sides, as we had been the day before. The village was totally destroyed—not a house left standing, not a tree unscarred. Dead chickens, pigs, and ducks lay everywhere, victims to the deadly spray of artillery shrapnel. Some of the bamboo-and-thatched huts were still burning, and the loud crackling and popping of the flaming wreckage could be heard from all directions. The white smoke from the rain-soaked, smoldering wreckage hung low over the village, stinging our throats and nostrils with the nauseating odor of burned flesh.

We moved on cautiously, expecting the worst. I was surprised to find myself suddenly standing in front of the hootch in which I had sought shelter during the previous day's battle. It was barely recognizable. Curious, I walked over to the concrete pillar and counted more than twenty small craters gouged out by the merciless bullets.

We continued to search the rubble for signs of the enemy. So far, there was no sign of the NVA soldiers. We picked our way through a splintered hedgerow and found what none of us had hoped for. There before us lay the slaughtered troopers from Delta Company—between twenty and thirty lifeless soldiers who had walked into the same ambush that we had triggered. We figured the only reason we had not been killed en masse was because the enemy soldiers had nervously sprung the ambush too early, thus allowing us the advantage of cover. These corpses lay on the edge of a small rice field; they obviously had been caught in the open and mowed down by deadly machine-gun fire. Their expressions were horrible and their skin had turned a ghostly white from lying out in the cold rain. We set up security while the 2nd Platoon wrapped the bodies in ponchos and carried them back to the schoolhouse.

When all the bodies were removed, we proceeded on slowly and soon came upon the area from which the NVA had fought. They had dug in well, with narrow trenches running between their fighting positions; this enabled them to move from one foxhole to another while remaining below ground level. We searched the area thoroughly and discovered many of the enemy dead over their weapons. Some were slumped over machine guns and mortar tubes, having been caught by the Cobra gunships or by a surprise barrage of artillery shells. We collected their weapons as we went, and the prize of the day was a small 61mm mortar tube with base plate and tripod. This mortar piece was small enough to be carried around, so we quickly decided to claim it for the company and barter the needed ammunition from the Marines. The Army did not use this particular weapon, but the Marines used 60mm mortars as part of their basic equipment and would have an ample supply of HE, illumination, and "Willie Peter" (white phosphorous) rounds. All we would need to obtain these mortar shells would be a few cases of beer, which would be a simple task for our crafty supply sergeant. Most of the other weapons we found were badly burned or blown to pieces by the artillery; still, we gathered up a pile of rifles and machine guns for shipment back to base camp.

As we moved on through the battered village, just leaving a small cluster of burned hootches, someone heard cries coming from beneath the rubble. We pulled away a pile of wreckage and found the opening to a bunker. Bill hollered, *"Lai day!"* ("Come here!") down the dark hole. As we all pointed our rifles toward the opening, a young boy, about eight years old, poked his head out and said, "GI numba one. Me no VC. Me Vietnam." I took off my gear and wedged myself through the small opening. An old woman and two small girls were also in the dark hole. I motioned for them to come out, and reached to help the mamasan toward the daylight. She groaned and pointed to her foot, which was wrapped in dirty, blood-soaked rags. The expression on her face told me she was in excruciating pain. The little girls scrambled out, and I carefully lifted the old woman out of the bunker. She was nothing but skin and bones and appeared to be in her eighties. Trying to get her out of those close quarters was like trying to push a chain. Two buddies grabbed her hands while I pushed with my shoulder against her bony buttocks. Together, we managed to free her from a would-be grave. She lay on the ground and nearly passed out as we unwrapped the rags. The poor old lady had nearly half her foot blown off by a piece of shrapnel. I'll never know why she had not died from blood loss. The children were scared to death, so Bud and a couple of other buddies tried to comfort them by handing out gum and talking softly to them in a language they could not understand. Doc Reems bandaged the woman's foot and gave her some morphine; I volunteered to carry her back to the schoolhouse for evacuation. I picked her up and cradled her in my arms, again surprised to find her so light. The children followed closely behind and spoke to her softly between their whimpering. It was almost a half mile back to the school, so I had to put her down a couple of times and rest. By the time we got there the morphine and exhaustion had caught up with her. She finally relaxed and laid her head on my shoulder. I left the four in good hands and returned to the company along with two other GIs who had accompanied me for security. We soon caught up and continued our search through the devastated village.

We were all astounded at the destruction of this small town. Not a single structure had escaped damage; hardly a tree or bamboo thicket was left standing. Dead animals littered the landscape and the stench of war was held close to the ground by the cold mist. We continued our sweep of Hai Lang, stopping at the far side of the village on the banks of a canal. Our search was completed and the enemy was nowhere to be found. He had suffered heavy casualties, but most had escaped during the night; only two young soldiers had been found hiding in a bunker. The thought of these men escaping to fight us again gave us a hatred for the North Vietnamese that we had not known before.

Orders came down that we were to assemble and wait for a crew of Seabees heading our way. Unbeknownst to us, the enemy had blown up every bridge and culvert along Highway One for three or four miles south of Hai Lang; the Seabees had been assigned the task of quickly replacing them with large, steel culvert pipe, and covering them with gravel. Our mission would be to provide security for the Seabees as they labored to rebuild the severed highway. They soon showed up with flatbeds loaded with culvert sections, dump trucks loaded with gravel, and a brand-new, enormous crane that looked as though it had just rolled off the assembly line. We rode slowly down the highway on their trucks, with a team of engineers before us sweeping for mines. We soon reached the first blown bridge and dismounted to form a wide circle around the work crew. The small canal was soon covered, and we moved down the road to the next site. Here we spread out in a large perimeter, dispersed on a network of dikes that stretched out among the giant rice fields on both sides of the road. Our visibility was good in all directions, so we felt somewhat secure in the vast sea of lush, green rice fields. Our positions had just settled down to allow half the men to indulge in a meal of C rats when a tremendous explosion echoed off the distant tree line.

I turned toward the sound in time to see several tandem wheels from the giant crane cartwheeling to heights of about 100 feet. The boom on the crane was bouncing up and down as cables whipped about in a wild frenzy. The blast blew culvert halves off a nearby flatbed; one bundle of them landed on a Seabee. Another engineer had his legs nearly torn off as a set of tandem wheels from the crane flew into him and flung him into the canal. The explosion had come from a large land mine planted in the soft earth around the blown-out bridge. The Seabees had missed it with their mine detectors, and it had detonated when the crane moved over it. The machine was a total wreck, with every major part twisted and distorted beyond repair. The Seabees extracted their wounded and pushed the crane off the highway with a bulldozer.

This was just another incident that instilled in us the warning that our foe must be respected: he fought dirty and would strike at us with whatever means available. We were learning fast that this was a war in which all stops had been pulled, and we would have to fight hard and dirty in order to stay one step ahead of our treacherous enemy.

The Seabees brought in a second crane, and we stayed with them for another day while they replaced the blown culverts. After completing this security mission, we learned that remnants of the NVA element we had fought in Hai Lang had holed up in a small village not far from there. We were to find them and clean up the remains of the battalion. We were wary of the danger that lay ahead, but anxious to strike back at those tough, little soldiers. As we approached the village from the north, we noticed a Huey flying low, with its machine guns clearing their throats into the village below. The chopper twisted and turned just above the trees, as the pilots maneuvered the craft so the gunners could address their targets. The familiar popping of AK47s could be heard above the drone of the chopper. The NVA were trying their best to shoot down the Huey, but it continued to fly low and spit tracers from its guns. We watched the Huey turn and fly away, trailing a thin line of black smoke. We heard later that our battalion commander, Colonel "P," had suffered two broken legs as bullets tore through the floor and struck him and another officer.

We moved forward along a road bordering a tremendous rice field and were told to hold up there and set up a blocking position for the village, which lay about a quarter of a mile to our front. B and C companies had choppered in on the far side of the village and were to sweep through it and push the NVA in our direction. It was late in the afternoon as we sat in the rain and listened to the staccato of the ensuing firefight. We were well out of the danger zone, but still instinctively ducked as stray bullets buzzed over our heads. Gunships circled the village like vultures, columns of smoke rose from burning hootches, and gunfire chattered over the lush rice fields as we watched a fierce battle unfold. We knew that death was occurring in a wholesale manner just inside the village, and there we were—just watching. It gave us an empty feeling to know that our comrades from Geronimo Battalion were fighting their hearts out and we could not help them. All we could do was sit and have another cigarette as though nothing was going on. We counted three medevacs, with telltale red crosses painted on their sides, fly in to evacuate the dead and wounded.

A sudden burst of nearby machine-gun fire sent us all scrambling for cover. Our positions had spotted an enemy soldier running aimlessly from the village. He must have crawled through the rice until he felt safe enough to get up and run along an elevated dike; he charged straight into one of our M60s and was killed in quick fashion.

The firefight continued until dark. Then the firing stopped as though a referee had blown the final whistle. Bravo and Charlie companies had withdrawn for the night to lick their wounds. We were ordered to dig in and remain there as a cordon against the escaping enemy. We moved to slightly higher ground, just to the other side of the road. Each position dug a fighting hole on the edge of the road, and mine chose a clear spot less than ten feet away from a nice, dry hootch. The rain had become heavier as darkness approached. We were ecstatic to think that at least two of us would get to sleep out of the rain; the third sat on the edge of the slowly filling foxhole and pulled his hour of guard.

I pulled the first watch and became thoroughly soaked as I stood in the foxhole for sixty minutes, staring into the black night that pressed up against my face. We couldn't see more than three feet in the darkness, and I felt a cold chill run up my back as I imagined those smiling, little soldiers from North Vietnam sneaking up on us, not making a sound in the wet foliage. My guard finally ended, and I crawled out of the foxhole and made my way over to the dark shadow of the hootch. Feeling my way around, I found Bud asleep just inside the wide door opening. The hootch had been evacuated by its owners because of the battle nearby, so we had it all to ourselves—or so we thought. I gave Bud my watch, and we exchanged a few words in the dark. I rolled up in my poncho liner and stretched out on the hard dirt floor. Cradling my rifle in one arm, I lay my head on my rucksack, enjoying the feeling of my poncho liner slowly removing the chill from my wet clothes. I laughed quietly when I heard Bud mumble a few profanities as his feet hit the five or six inches of water in the bottom of our foxhole. Rolling over slightly to get my weight off the maps folded up in my thigh pockets, my back pushed up against what seemed like a bamboo fence woven together by rope. I reached out with my hand to figure out just what it was I was sleeping against, and my hand went through an opening in the bamboo. Horror rose within me as I touched something big and warm and hairy. It moved slightly and grunted as though it was about to devour me for disturbing its sleep. I quickly withdrew my hand and reached for my rifle. Another grunt made me realize that I was bedded down less than twelve inches from a large hog, caged up in a small pen inside the hootch. In Vietnam, it was a common custom for farmers to keep valuable livestock in their houses so they would always know where they were. I lay still for a few moments and surveyed the situation. The hog grunted softly once more, as though to assure me that she was docile, so I slowly stretched back out beside her and slept like a baby for the next two hours.

Daylight brought us all back to our foxholes as rifle fire alerted us to an early-morning push by Bravo and Charlie companies. They were moving back through the village, firing into bunkers and tree lines that had hidden enemy troops just a few hours before. The surviving NVA had again escaped under cover of darkness and were nowhere near the small village, which now lay deserted and in ruins. After a quick break-fast of C's, most of us shaved with a helmet full of cold, dirty water from the nearby rice paddy before saddling up to move back toward Hai Lang. Civilians had begun to drift back into the previous day's battle site, and we passed them as they trudged back toward their homes to begin picking up the pieces. We stopped an old man pushing a cart full of fresh bread to barter with him for his wares. He smiled and jabbered loudly at us through a wiry mustache and goatee. Several of us bought the sweet-smelling bread from him and began to devour it, washing it down with iodine-flavored water from our canteens. I was almost finished with mine when a fellow GI spit out a mouthful of bread, cursing the old man who had sold it to us. He showed us his half-eaten loaf, and there among the air holes perforating the bread were two, small, white worms. We all looked at each other with disgust and disbelief until someone commented that "a little protein never hurt anyone."

That night our platoon was ordered to move around Hai Lang after dark and set up an ambush in another small village about a mile away. After about two hours of stop-and-go checks with our compasses, we made it to our destination. For some reason Lieutenant Hernandez was extremely nervous, which made all of us jump at every noise. Sergeant Hands, sensing the problem, quietly moved among us and soon had things running smoothly again. It turned out to be an uneventful night. Our ambush ended at dawn, when we pulled out of the village and headed back toward the company perimeter.

Our CO greeted us with the news that we would be clearing another village that day; there had been reports of small pockets of VC and NVA working from its boundaries. We reached this village around noon and had swept through more than half of it when we reached a large rice paddy located within its center. We fanned out and moved across it at a quick pace. Before our platoon had completed its crossing, a VC mortar team started dropping 80mm shells on us from somewhere up ahead. Rounds were dropping at random from one side of the rice field to the other, with no set pattern to their firing. We all started running for the nearest tree line, about 100 yards away. I was one of the last to reach the tree line, which I hit at full speed.

As I followed the rest of my buddies into the undergrowth bordering the paddy, I felt something grab my leg as though I had snagged the cuff of my pants on barbed wire. My momentum, and the adrenaline pumping through me, pulled my leg free, and I threw myself down beside "Handy" Matthews as another mortar round crashed nearby. As we lay there catching our breath, I noticed a burning sensation in my left leg. I sat up and discovered that my leg was covered with blood from the knee down. There was a small tear in my pants and protruding from my leg was a stick that had broken off in splinters. I pulled up my pant leg to stare unbelievably at a punji stake embedded in my calf. It had entered from the front of my leg, glanced off the shinbone, and then gone halfway through my calf muscle. Handy yelled for a medic and Doc Reems crawled over to us while the last of the mortar shells exploded harmlessly in the rice paddy. The stake had pierced about three inches of my flesh, and was protruding enough for Doc to get a firm grip on it with his tweezers. He quickly jerked out the sliver of bamboo and proceeded to pull all sorts of paraphernalia from his medic's kit. He soaked the tip of a long-stemmed cotton swab in some orange solution and without warning jammed it clear to the back of the hole in my leg. I cursed him loudly. Being the good friend that he was, he just laughed and continued to work on my leg. The punji stake was old and had probably been there, waiting for me, for several months. Because of this, it was hard to tell whether it had been dipped in human or animal feces, a common practice for the VC. Doc cleaned the wound again and then wrapped my lower leg with a sterile bandage. I could have asked for a medevac chopper to take me back to LZ Jane, but I chose to stay with the company, since we had just learned of orders to be choppered into a village where there was confirmed enemy.

We secured the area and called in artillery on the section of the village where the mortar had been fired. Chopper loads were divided up and dispersed along the large paddy, and since the 3rd Platoon would be lifted out last, we settled down for a smoke. Our sortie held six Hueys, and it would take three trips to move our whole company to the new AO. The first load was lifted out and dropped into a hot LZ. We had put "long john" antennas on our radios, so we could maintain contact with the 1st Platoon. They were getting hit from all sides, having been dropped off in a rice field surrounded by the hostile village. One chopper was immediately hit by a .51-caliber machine gun, and one of its door-gunners was killed instantly, pinned up against his seat by several machine-gun slugs. We also picked up the radio call for a medevac to lift out one KIA and five WIA. The choppers soon came back, minus the crippled bird, and picked up the 2nd Platoon to carry them off to the battle. They chose a different landing zone this time and were hit even harder, with one Huey shot down and three more troopers wounded. Our turn was next, and the tension mounted while we waited more than an hour for additional choppers to fly in from a different base camp. We hid in the edge of the tree line, listening to our comrades call each other for assistance. To make matters worse, it started raining again.

We checked and rechecked our weapons, knowing we would soon be using them. Finally, we heard our chopper sortie drawing closer in the misty sky. Smoke was thrown to identify our position, and five slicks flew in, flattening the tall green rice plants as they hovered just long enough for us to scramble on. The engines strained to lift the added weight, and we flew low over the rice field to gain speed. The approaching tree line was coming on fast, and at the last moment, the pilot pulled back on the stick and vaulted us over the barrier. We figured our flight would take about ten minutes, but time passed as we continued to fly in a wide circle that took us out over the Gulf of Tonkin. We were flying at about 2,000 feet, and several soldiers, including Bill Rollins, were sitting in the open doorways with their legs hanging out. The choppers made a sudden banking turn and Bill was almost thrown out. Only his rucksack saved him. As Bill's feet caught the runners, the rucksack hung on the door frame for the split second Bud and I needed to grab it and drag him back into the chopper. Bill's face was colorless as he hollered his gratitude over the droning engine and scrambled to a safer seat. Bud and I couldn't help laughing at the way Bill had flailed around like a headless chicken.

We continued to fly in wide circles; a door-gunner yelled that we were going to have to refuel. We flew to Quang Tri base camp for more "av-gas" and learned from a pilot that we couldn't land at the village because of the hot LZ. We would have to wait while the rest of our company battled it out with the North Vietnamese. Taking off again, we heard that we finally were going in, landing about a half mile from the village. This meant we would have to approach the village in the open, picking our way through hostile territory as we tried to link up with the rest of Alpha Company. The Hueys touched down, and we raced for a large graveyard that would give us protection as we moved toward the village. Graveyards in Vietnam were built on the edges of rice fields and were dotted with large mounds of earth or small crescent-shaped concrete fences encircling every grave. We often used these areas for night positions or for moving in the open, since the mounds and circular tombstones provided cover in case of an attack.

As we entered the village, everything was quiet except for an occasional rifle shot. We spread out and began cautiously working our way from one hootch to another. Ken Fryer and I walked around the rear of a large family bunker built beside a hootch—practically every family had built bunkers in case they were suddenly caught up in the jaws of war. The NVA rarely fought from these bunkers, but instead built their own smaller "spider holes" concealed in thick undergrowth. As Ken and I walked past this bunker, I noticed a rifle barrel coming out of the opening on the far side. It looked like a periscope rising from some unknown depth, and a head of black hair followed behind it. I hollered, "Look out!" and dove for a fresh mound of dirt in the yard. Everyone scrambled for cover as the enemy soldier swung toward us and sprayed the area with his AK47. Ken also leaped behind this pile of dirt, which was barely big enough for one, much less two. The NVA soldier reloaded and sprayed again as Mike Brinson cranked up his M60 from a nearby drainage ditch. Ken and I were caught in the open with no place to go as bullets tore away at our dirt pile. We were soon covered with the damp earth being kicked up by bullets. Stretched out flat on our stomachs with our faces against the ground, it was impossible to jump up and fire back. Each time the little soldier withdrew to reload, a machine gun from somewhere behind him would open up on us. This continued for several long minutes. Ken and I then decided to lob a grenade toward the bunker, but since we were unable to see the bunker entrance, our grenade simply bounced past and exploded in the hedge-row beyond. Sergeant Hands had moved up along with Lieutenant Hernandez, but they could get no closer than fifty yards due to the enemy machine-gunner.

Our situation looked gloomy as the two enemy soldiers took turns firing at us. Someone from behind threw another grenade, which landed on top of the large bunker and rolled down toward Ken and me before exploding. Our precious mound of earth was growing smaller as bullets continued to chip away handfuls of dirt. It was then that I heard Bud's voice yelling for someone to give him covering fire. Several troopers had managed to crawl up to the drainage canal, and they began laying down a field of fire as Bud raced toward the hootch by the enemy bunker. He disappeared inside, and in a few seconds he raced out, firing his rifle with one hand and clutching a grenade in the other. Leaping on top of the bunker, he threw the grenade inside, while the enemy machine gun to our front chewed up the hootch beside him. That enabled Ken and me to fire back at the machine-gunner. Bud raced back for cover. Our attention quickly swung back to the bunker as the scared little soldier tossed the grenade back outside; it exploded in the yard. Bud jumped up and again ran toward the bunker, with a trip flare in one hand and a grenade in the other. As we fired our rifles to hold down the machine-gun fire, Bud jumped back up on the bunker and threw the trip flare in first, following it with a grenade. He tried this approach, hoping that the NVA would be distracted by the spewing hot flare and would not notice the hand grenade as it rolled down the entrance. To our surprise, the hand grenade was tossed outside again, where it exploded harmlessly. The deciding factor was the white, acrid smoke from the trip flare, which finally forced the enemy soldier from his hole. He crawled blindly from the bunker and staggered toward the hootch, where Mike Brinson cut him in two with his M60. Bud ran forward and put a round through his head to finish him off.

For a split second, I stared with pity at the bloody carcass of the young North Vietnamese. He no longer suffered. He no longer was scared. He had fought alone and died alone. I couldn't help but feel a bit of respect for this individual, who only moments before had tried to take my life.

Then we turned our attention to the machine-gun nest. Scrambling to my knees, I crawled around the hootch where I could get a better view of the incoming fire. Others spread out and began to circle around from the left flank as I crawled forward under the cover of some low-lying bushes and peered around a hedgerow. To my surprise, there were two NVA soldiers racing down a path and carrying a machine gun. Jumping up, I fired on full automatic and watched one's head fly apart like a watermelon rolling off the back of a farm truck. The other escaped, leaving behind his comrade and the Chi-Com (Chinese Communist) machine gun.

I had witnessed death before and accepted it; I had been indirectly involved in killing enemy soldiers, without seeing them actually fall on the battlefield; and I had experienced the emptiness of seeing a buddy killed before my very eyes. I had never once questioned the reason for killing another human being in the fright of battle, but this was the first time I had watched the enemy die at the end of my rifle barrel. Emotions welled within me that I will never be able to express fully. I had always heard that you would soon forget about taking the life of an enemy soldier, but this was not true. I am convinced that those who knowingly killed on the battlefield had high respect for those unknown soldiers who were placed there for the same reason. In the din and confusion of a firefight, it's easy to kill another soldier. It's those long hours spent alone on guard in a foxhole that gnaw at your guts and send the mind into spirals as you wonder who that person really was and what his family would go through. But I molded my emotions to accept the fact that I would kill again, probably many times more, and would gladly do so in order to survive.

We quickly assembled to move on toward the rest of the company and had gone only a short distance when Tom Cashion walked up on an occupied spider hole. Tom was a grenadier and carried only an M79 grenade launcher, which was no good in close combat. He rounded a hedgerow and stood face-to-face with a petrified NVA soldier, staring back at him from within his fighting position. "Cash" instinctively raised his grenade launcher and fired from less than five feet away, striking the enemy soldier in the head and killing him instantly. The projectile did not explode, because it was made to travel several meters before becoming armed. We began to move forward once more. The dreaded "whump, whump" of a mortar tube echoed through the village. From about 300 yards away an enemy mortar team was walking rounds in our direction, and each explosion was getting closer. We raced for a lily-covered canal we had just passed and dove into about four feet of water to seek cover from the deadly shells. I shivered not only from the cold water but from the eerie sound the mortar shells made as they whined over our heads. I later learned that Mike Brinson and Joey Miller had the hell scared out of them when a dud mortar shell landed between them and sank into the soft mud of the canal bank.

Friendly artillery soon quieted the mortar firing, and we crawled from the canal to resume our search for the 1st and 2nd platoons. Scattered fighting resumed as we worked our way forward, clearing out small pockets of resistance along the way. We soon linked up with the rest of the company and continued to push through the village. The enemy was pulling out as darkness approached, so we withdrew to the graveyard to set up a night defensive perimeter. We dug in and settled down while cold rain continued to fall. The monsoon season had definitely arrived. Life in Vietnam was now not only a matter of trying to stay alive, but trying to stay dry and warm. None of us had been totally dry in several days, and our feet were becoming a matter of concern since we continually trudged in mud and water and never allowed them to dry.

As darkness crept over us, we sat huddled together in our foxholes quietly talking of the day's battles. We wondered about our wounded and were especially concerned about Terry Hamrickson, who had been shot and put on a medevac in critical condition. As we sat and talked I noticed that my leg was throbbing from the punjistake wound. I had forgotten about it during the excitement of the firefight, and now I realized that the bandages were wet and muddy from the canal. I left our position and crawled over to Doc Reems. He cleaned the wound and rewrapped it. During the night my leg became worse. I ended up pulling several hours of watch, unable to sleep because of the throbbing pain.

When morning came, Doc redressed my leg and announced that I was going back to base camp—the hole in my calf had begun to fester and turn an angry red. I had to wait several hours before a chopper was dispatched due to the fog and rain. Once the weather subsided, the chopper flew in, and I scrambled aboard for a cold ride back to LZ Jane. The rain was still coming down, and the base camp had been transformed into a giant bog. Thick, dark mud was everywhere, and every man, vehicle, tent, and piece of equipment had taken on a brown hue instead of the usual army green. I hobbled over to the aid station for treatment before trying to find A Company's camp tent. Entering the aid station, I was greeted by Doc Bell's assistant, a tall, overweight, black sergeant who looked like Buddha. He had a tremendous beer gut that lapped over his belt; a bald, shiny head; and a friendly personality that reminded me of a used car salesman. When he unwrapped my leg, the infection oozed in a steady stream. He cursed at me for waiting so long to have it properly attended to. He cleaned out the wound with a large swab, just as Doc Reems had done, but this time he made two neat incisions across the hole with a scalpel in order to allow better drainage. I received a couple of shots for the infection and some pills to take for the pain. Then I asked for instructions on how to find A Company.

I was greeted at the tent by several of my buddies, who were eager to hear news about those still out in the boonies. Most of these troopers had rear-area jobs: supply workers, clerks, mess cooks, plus three or four injured soldiers like me. There weren't enough cots to go around, so I ended up sleeping on a mound of duffel bags piled in one corner. I didn't really mind because it put me farther away from the slimy quagmire that flowed in under the tent walls.

My first night back in base camp I was sure I would finally get a full night's sleep without having to pull guard, but during the middle of the night we were hit with half a dozen 122mm rockets, which sent us racing through the mud for cover. Slipping and falling, I followed everyone else, since they seemed to know where the bunkers were located. To my surprise they led me through the darkness to a trash sump half full of water and floating garbage. I hesitated briefly as I heard them hit the water, but a rocket exploding nearby sent me leaping into the dark hole. I landed on what appeared to be something solid, but it turned out to be a piece of cardboard floating in about two feet of water. Losing my balance, I plunged face first among hundreds of C-ration cans floating about in the cold, muddy water. After the rocket attack, we found our way back to the tent, and the company clerk gave me a pair of his dry fatigues, since I was wearing the only pair I owned. After changing, I headed out into the darkness to find the aid station. My bandage was wet again, and I was afraid to wear it for the rest of the night. I had to wait for a couple of hours while Doc Bell worked on some minor shrapnel wounds received during the rocket attack.

The next day I sat around and read old *Playboy* magazines and wrote letters to my family and friends. The rain picked up its pace, and I couldn't help but think of my buddies in the 3rd Platoon out there somewhere in that miserable weather. Mail call was held and it was one I would never forget. I received three boxes of Valentine candy, a few letters, and most surprising of all, a wedding invitation from one of my best friends back home. I jokingly asked the first sergeant for a three-day pass in order to attend, but he just mumbled something and looked at me as though I was crazy.

Also arriving, via the mail truck, were four new replacements for A

Company, sent over from the battalion TOC. They wandered up to our tent looking very lost. You could tell they were replacements by the way they wore their gear. Every piece of equipment the Army had issued was hanging from their pistol belts and rucksacks; it looked as though it would all fall off the first time they had to run for cover or dive behind a thicket of bamboo. We referred to them as "cherries," the common term for those who had not yet lost their virginity to combat. These fresh troops seemed a little embarrassed at their lack of experience, but all of us knew it wouldn't be long before they were seasoned veterans. After a few minutes of awkward introductions, we took them inside the tent and helped them rearrange their equipment in a more practical fashion and discard some things that only added extra weight.

Later in the afternoon we came under another rocket attack. This time I headed for a small sandbag bunker that had been built on top of the ground due to the heavy rains. Several others had the same idea, and the bunker quickly became crowded. One of the cherries was crouched in the doorway of the bunker, his back exposed to the rockets exploding within the perimeter. One landed close by, throwing up giant chunks of rock and earth, and a large piece of wet clay hit him in the back, sending him sprawling over the rest of us. It did nothing more than knock the breath from him, and when he regained his senses, he laughed, telling us he should no longer be called a cherry. Several more rockets screamed into the base camp, and one exploded just under the front fender of a jeep parked on a nearby hill. The jeep was thrown more than fifty feet into the air and landed on its wheels in the exact place it had been sitting. The explosion had twisted it in the middle, so the front wheels pointed in one direction and the rear wheels in another. The jeep sat there in a mangled heap with its turn signals blinking as curious GIs gathered around to stare in amazement.

I stayed at base camp for three or four more days while my leg healed, and boredom set in. All I had to do was stay out of the rain, play poker, and write letters. My leg was healing well, so I asked the first sergeant if I could take a supply "log ship" chopper and rejoin the company. He informed me that the company was on its way back to base camp and would spend a couple of days here before returning to the field. Three large Chinook helicopters (often called "shithooks" by the infantry soldiers) soon landed outside the concertina wire, and off-loaded A Company. I went out to greet them, taking the cherries with me so they could be assigned to the platoons in need of more manpower. The CO assigned Rob Scott from California to the 3rd Platoon, and I escorted him over to meet Lieutenant Hernandez and Sergeant Hands. He was then assigned to our squad. After introductions, we quickly dubbed him "Scotty."

The platoons were assigned to certain sectors of the perimeter. After finding out where the "Third Herd" would be, I hurried back to the tent to get my gear and join them. We quickly strung our ponchos over the metal frame at our sleeping position. Each bunker had one of these positions built just behind it—a shallow hole dug in the ground with sandbags piled around and steel fence stakes over the hole. Ponchos could be fastened over the stakes to provide a makeshift roof. The poncho roof worked well, but the holes still filled with water, making sleeping very uncomfortable if not impossible.

Later on that day the rain came down in buckets and cut our visibility to zero. It had gotten cold, and our wet fatigues clung to our bodies and wrinkled our skin. I shared a position with Bud, Ken, and Scotty, and three of us tried to sleep while the fourth sat like a cold stone on the edge of the bunker. Four or five inches of cold, muddy water lay in the bottom of the sleeping position. At first we tried to sleep sitting up, then decided we might as well lie down. Lying separately in the cold, wet pool of water, we finally said, "the hell with it," and curled up like dogs in order to share our body heat.

When morning came we tried to warm ourselves and dry our clothes by building small fires from ammo boxes. The rain continued to fall, so our fires simply smoldered and went out. News came that we would soon be leaving LZ Jane for an unknown destination near the coast. We were elated to be leaving the mud and misery of base camp.

We saddled up and moved outside the wire perimeter only to sit and wait another two hours in the cold drizzle. Waiting had become second nature to us over the past two months. We patiently settled into small poker games or just stretched out on the muddy turf for a lonesome smoke or a short nap. The hours slowly dragged by until the sharp voice of our CO barked out that our choppers would arrive in ten minutes. Several Hueys flew in, picked up our whole company, and flew us off to an unknown destination. We headed east toward the coast, starting our descent over vast plains of white sand hills covered with brush, stunted from the brisk coastal winds.

I had been sitting in the doorway during the flight and as we descended, I swung my legs out to stand on the skids. This was a common practice when we were coming into a landing zone, since it gave us an edge when departing the chopper if it should happen to come under fire. I was standing on the skids and leaning out while holding on to the door frame with one hand. At about 100 feet off the ground, the chopper next to ours opened up with its M60s and sprayed tracers under our bird. The rounds appeared to be just inches below my feet and the thought of being shot off of that chopper frightened me to death. I figured that we were being fired at and might possibly abort the landing, so I proceeded to scramble back inside the chopper. I was all knees, butt, and elbows as I clawed for a foothold on the edge of the door, peeling all the bark from my shins. I must have put on quite a show, because everyone was laughing—even the door-gunner. It turned out that the gunners on several choppers were firing at random into the brush below in order to scare out anything that might have been waiting for us.

We landed, raced for cover, and lay still as the Hueys ascended and flew away, covering us with a light dusting of moist sand. It was well into the afternoon when word came down that we would spend the night in the sand dunes and proceed to our destination the next morning. We established a company perimeter and started digging in before darkness fell. No traces of the enemy had been seen, so we felt rather secure—we appeared to be the only signs of life for miles around.

When our perimeter was set, three or four LPs (listening posts) of three men each were sent out in all directions to lay low in the bushes and provide early warning in case of attack. About halfway through the night, during my second watch, one of our LPs was hit by a squad of North Vietnamese soldiers. The three troopers managed to fight them off, but one soldier caught a rifle slug in the throat. His two buddies dragged him back to the perimeter, where a medevac was called. The chopper soon flew in to extract the dying GI, and I watched as one of our people held a strobe light for the chopper to home in on. Just before touchdown, the pilot turned on his approach lights in order to make his landing, then immediately blacked out his lights again as several grunts and medics carried out the wounded soldier.

The engines labored as the pilot lifted the whirling machine into the black sky. His line of flight brought him directly over my position, and I turned my face upward and strained to detect the huge silhouette as it raced away toward the 22nd Surgical Hospital at Phu Bai. When the chopper was directly over me, the sky suddenly was laced by red tracers as enemy gunners to my front tried to shoot down the moving target they could detect only by sound. Hearing the popping of their AKs above the noise of the chopper, I instinctively dove to the bottom of my foxhole. Realizing they were not shooting at us, I stood up and took a bead on the origin of a continuous line of tracers coming from the sand dunes in front of me. With my M16 on "rock and roll," I covered up the muzzle flashes with a full magazine of tracers, which I always used at night simply as a psychological edge. The firing immediately ceased, and I smiled with satisfaction knowing I had been the one to stop the enemy gunner. I felt proud to have helped the medevac escape, and quietly said "You're welcome!" as I stared into the darkness toward the fading engine noise.

With the NVA at our front door, we pulled 100 percent alert for the rest of the night, which meant no one would sleep but would stand alert in their foxholes. The night passed without further incident. Dawn covered us with a cool mist that continued to hover and slowly soaked our clothes. As the light brightened, soldiers began to climb from their fighting positions and move around. Some ate cold C rations; others fired up a heat tablet for a hot cup of coffee or cocoa. Still others chose to perform minor duties of personal hygiene like brushing teeth or washing their faces with a handful of water from their canteens. None of us had bathed in several weeks, and our fatigues had almost grown to our bodies. Bud finished a can of C's and mentioned that he had to go relieve himself. His next act was a mistake that taught him a lesson he would never forget: he left his rifle laying across his gear when he walked a few meters to the top of a small sand dune to drop his drawers and squat. He had nearly completed his business when an enemy soldier cut down on him with an AK. Three or four rounds kicked up sand just beneath his buttocks. Bud jumped like a frightened deer, as we all dove for cover and immediately started returning fire toward the general direction of the incoming rounds. When the firing subsided, all of us broke into side-splitting laughter as Bud came low-crawling back to our position with his pants still down around his ankles. He was lucky, and he knew it. He jokingly stated that he wouldn't have to defecate for at least another month.

We moved out parallel with the coast and walked until we reached an area of large sand dunes some thirty to fifty feet high. We encircled one large sand hill and were told we would be setting up a defensive perimeter for a small fire base. A Chinook soon flew in and off-loaded a team of mortar men and all of their equipment. Another Chinook dropped a sling load of concertina wire and bundles of sandbags. The rest of the day was spent building bunkers and stringing wire. By nightfall we had established a small fire base, which to my knowledge never had a name.

Just after dark, Lieutenant Hernandez came over to my position and told me to choose two men and take an LP to the next ridge line, about a quarter of a mile away. No one in his right mind wanted to leave the perimeter after dark in this enemy-infested no-man's-land. Everyone knew what was coming when I looked around to pick the lucky two who would go with me. I chose Ric Ricart and Tony Briley. Being the good soldiers they always were, they simply said, "Okay, let's go!" and started preparing their gear. I coordinated our position with the FO (forward observer for artillery) and checked with the mortar teams in case we needed their support. We would travel light, taking only rifles, ammo, grenades, and a radio. We would stay awake the entire night so no poncho liners would be needed; normally we would pull two up and one asleep, but this area was too treacherous to let even one get a nap. Bud and Fast Herm went with us to the concertina wire to pull apart the coils so we could pass through and close them as we departed. I made a quick radio check and informed the company CP (control point) that "Lima Papa-3" was on its way and would be calling in a sitrep every hour. They acknowledged my call, and I quickly adjusted the squelch on the PRC-25 radio strapped to my back.

We moved out in a column with about five meters between us. I led the way and Ric brought up the rear. The rain had stopped briefly, but the night was cool and black. The tension soon brought a cold sweat to the three of us as our nerves drew taut. It took nearly an hour to reach our destination because we slowly made a wide circle to check out terrain features in case we needed to escape during the night. Finding a thick growth of shrubs, we settled in for a long night, hoping we had traveled unnoticed. We sat for hours without saying a word except to call in a situation report in a faint whisper.

About one or two o'clock in the morning, a nearby metallic sound stopped my heart. I knew Tony and Ric had heard it also, because they immediately lifted their rifles toward the sound. Something made another clanking noise and this time we heard voices speaking in Vietnamese. More sounds brought us to our knees. We determined that several enemy soldiers were moving into our immediate area and setting up a mortar tube. We couldn't see them through the thick brush, but it sounded as though they were thirty or forty meters away. The three of us were frozen in our tracks, and I knew Tony and Ric were waiting for a decision. I quietly slid my arms through the radio straps and keyed the receiver. Someone on the other end acknowledged with, "This is Alpha Six. Go ahead."

With the volume down low and the phone receiver to my ear, only I could hear the transmission. I whispered, "This is Lima Papa-3. Our situation is red. Over." The voice came back: "Acknowledge—situation red. Do you need illumination? Over."

"Negative."

"Do you need assistance? Over."

"Negative. We're about to fire up enemy troops and return to home base. Over."

With that I touched Tony and Ric and held out a grenade. They got the message and reached into their pockets. We stood up, rifles in one hand and grenades in the other. With a silent signal we pulled the pins and threw the grenades toward the voices chattering in the dark. We ducked behind the bushes to wait for the explosions. It seemed like an eternity before five seconds went by, but then three loud explosions echoed over the sand dunes. We leaped up and fired full automatic toward the target. After emptying our magazines, I yelled, "Let's go," but Tony and Ric were already hauling ass toward home. I fell in behind them at a full gait, yelling to remind them to use the running password when we approached the perimeter. This was a prearranged code word used at night in case we had to move back toward friendly positions; it identified us so our own people wouldn't open up on us or blow a claymore mine in our faces.

When we were about halfway home, I started shouting the password as we ran. "Geronimo! Geronimo! Don't shoot! Don't shoot—Geronimo!" The three of us yelled as we ran at full speed. Suddenly a low-mounded grave loomed out of the darkness and cut my feet out from under me as though they had been grabbed by a ghostly hand. I tried to catch myself but fell hard, burying my face in the cold, wet sand. The radio on my back slammed into my head like a hammer, and the small control knobs punched holes in my scalp. I tried to get to my feet, but my knees buckled like those of a newborn colt. Ric and Tony heard me fall and turned around to help me. Finding me sprawled on the ground they grabbed my arms and pulled me up, and the three of us continued our flight back toward the company perimeter.

We shouted again, "Don't shoot—Geronimo! Don't shoot—Geronimo! Geronimo!"

Bud was waiting for us at the wire, yelling, "Come on in, Charlie! Over here, Charlie!" We found the opening and raced in under cover of our own guns. It was a great relief to be back within the perimeter, and I made my way toward the CP to report what had happened. I had the medics put salve on the cuts on the back of my head and then tried to get a couple of hours sleep.

The next morning, Ric, Tony, and I led our platoon out to the LP site to see what we could find, but there were only several footprints and a whole lot of blood. Finding nothing of significance, we swept across several ridges of sand dunes and approached a small village. It was deserted, which made us nervous, but a thorough sweep of the area turned up nothing. We returned to the fire base late in the afternoon, only to learn that we would be tearing down the bunkers and departing the next morning. This didn't surprise us—the continuing Tet Offensive kept us hopping from one area of operation to another, and fire bases were short lived in this highly mobile conflict.

As we packed our gear the next morning, a hard rain soaked us and the snow-white sand adhered to everything it touched. We were covered with sand, and many of us wrapped our rifles in fatigue shirts to keep the grit from choking down the sensitive bolts and trigger mechanisms.

The depressing rain also seemed to bring bad news on this particular day: Sergeant Hands informed us that he would be leaving. He had kept this from us so as not to contribute to our low morale. His latest hitch was about to expire, so he was going home to Fayetteville, North Carolina, and re-up while he was there. He would be gone for about thirty days, but assured us he was coming back. We all dreaded the thought of having a different platoon sergeant, since Eddie Hands had been with us since we formed at Fort Campbell, and he was like a big brother to us. Even Lieutenant Hernandez seemed depressed, since he often relied on the strength and expertise of this professional soldier.

Sergeant First Class Eddie Hands was picked up by a Huey later that morning as we prepared to be extracted by Chinooks. When we said good-bye, he once again told us to keep our heads down and that he would definitely be back. Our large, double-rotored choppers soon lumbered in and lifted us off to a new area of operation.

This new AO, named Quang Dien, was paradise compared to the sand dunes. It consisted of villages untouched by the war and inhabited by scores of women and children. We landed at the edge of a large rice field and moved over to the banks of the Song Bo River. The river was bordered by a dirt road running parallel with its north bank; dozens of hootches and shops lined the high side of the road. We moved in among the hootches and were told to hold up and take a break. Mike Brinson, Ken Fryer, and I went over to a small roadside market run by a young woman. We spoke to her and sat down for a rest in front of the tables covered with goods. I had just taken a drink from my canteen and lit a cigarette when a small baby boy tottered out from behind a table and jabbered excitedly to me. He had on nothing but a bright-blue shirt— Vietnamese babies wore no diapers or pants. He had large brown eyes and black fuzzy hair that stood up on his head like the down on a baby chick. I spoke to him and tried to coax him toward me with a piece of gum. When he waddled over, I grabbed him and lifted him on to my lap. His mother seemed nervous, so I smiled at her and stroked his fuzzy head. As I bounced the cute little fellow on my knees, with Mike and Ken watching and laughing, he suddenly peed all over me. Ken and Mike rolled on the ground in hysterics as the mother scooped up her baby, scolding him profusely. I simply removed my fatigue shirt, rinsed it out in the muddy river water, and put it right back on.

We moved on down the river to a less inhabited area and were told we could take a two-hour break in order to bathe. We were delighted to have a chance to remove the several weeks' worth of dirt and sweat that encrusted our bodies. Half of us immediately stripped and plunged into the cool water, while the other half pulled guard over us from the bank and waited their turn. We carried bars of soap in our packs; without washcloths, however, the soap was not getting the job done. Someone from our ingenious bunch thought of pressing the wet soap in the river bottom and coating it with sand. This did the trick—the sand helped remove the dirt caked on us like an extra layer of skin.

As we were enjoying this first bath in more than a month, tragedy struck. Ken Fryer had swum out to the middle of the river, and he was suddenly swept up by a vicious current. He floundered for an instant, then disappeared. He was at least fifty feet from the rest of us when he went under, and the current was lengthening that distance every second. Four of us tore out after him as his head bobbed up farther downstream. Scotty and I reached him simultaneously and grabbed for his flailing arms. Ken was a young black soldier who was as strong as an ox. When he felt us grab him, he latched on to our heads and pushed both of us under. As I was being held down, I realized it would be a losing battle to fight both Ken and the current, which was spinning the three of us around like a top. My lungs were at the exploding point, so I instinctively turned my efforts toward self-preservation. With one last ounce of strength, I tore away from his grip, burst through the surface, and sucked fresh air into my screaming lungs. Scotty also had managed to escape the death grip. Four other GIs had taken over the task of trying to save Ken, so Scotty and I rolled over on our backs and floated for a few seconds to regain our strength. Luck was on our side. The river made a sharp turn and the swirling water ran over a sandbar extending halfway toward the southern bank; the seven of us washed up on the sand bank. Several of our buddies jumped in to help us out—they had run down the bank following us, stripping off their boots and clothes as they ran. Ken was nearly done for and had to be carried from the water. We all lay naked on the bank, gasping the cool, refreshing air and mumbling profanities about how close we had come to drowning.

We stayed along the river bank that night and moved upstream the next day to help guard the An Lo Bridge, which allowed Highway One to span the river. The North Vietnamese had blown out two sections of the bridge during the opening hours of Tet, but army engineers had constructed a makeshift span that allowed traffic to resume its normal flow. Security was necessary in order to keep the bridge from being blown again, so an infantry company was required to conduct constant guard and pull patrols in the surrounding villages. An old French fortress was on the north bank of the river; we used the concrete bunkers here as sleeping quarters and pulled guard from the sandbag positions built by GIs who had been there before us.

We stayed at the bridge for a couple of days and again got a chance to bathe in the river. One afternoon a few of us were bathing in the shallow waters near the bridge as several old mamasans washed clothes on the rocks nearby. We were all buck naked, but thought nothing of it since it was common custom for men and children to bathe publicly. As we were leisurely enjoying our bath, a chopper flew over, then made a sharp turn to fly back over us again. After a couple of passes, it landed on the bank, blowing most of our clothes into the water. A colonel jumped out and waved us over. It was a comical sight as we waded from the river and saluted him while wearing nothing at all. He demanded to know who was in charge, and I almost laughed out loud as Lieutenant Hernandez sheepishly stepped forward and saluted again. We all stood at attention as this stern-faced colonel proceeded to bless out the terribly embarrassed lieutenant. We were ordered never to bathe in the nude again, especially in a public area. This order, however, would soon be broken, since no one really seemed to care except this one particular "base camp desk jockey."

That night, the 3rd Platoon was given a mission that put fear in our hearts. We were to leave the bridge after dark and follow Highway One about two miles until we reached a small village. We were then instructed to sweep through the village and search the hootches for VC suspects. This was something new to us—we were not used to dealing with the people after dark. Moving through an unfamiliar village gave the VC and NVA an advantage over us. We were susceptible to ambushes because the VC usually knew every move we made. Local sympathizers relayed information with lightning speed, using different signals to warn each other that we were in the area. One of the most common was firing three shots into the air. When we heard the familiar three shots, we expected either a vacant village or a possible ambush.

We gathered at the bridge just after dark and received our final instructions. Weapons were checked, camouflage grease was applied, radio frequencies were cleared, and those last cigarettes of the evening were savored, down to the last possible drag. We moved out in a column and walked for a short distance along the highway. When the first large rice paddy appeared, our point veered out and moved our column some fifty meters from the highway so we walked parallel to it as it snaked through hamlets and graveyards. Movement was slow because precaution was taken before each tree line and hamlet—we were motioned to get down as two GIs moved ahead and searched out these areas of potential danger.

About a mile away from the bridge, we ran into problems we had never trained for. We were in the process of crossing a large rice field when the drone of chopper engines approached from the rear. It sounded like more than one chopper. As the noise drew closer we turned to see a frightening sight. A small OH-6 Cayuse helicopter was flying low over Highway One, scanning the terrain on either side of the road with powerful floodlights. Some 200 yards behind in total darkness lurked a Cobra gunship with its miniguns and rockets poised to annihilate anything that might appear in the searchlights to its front. This tactic was called "bird dogging," and it had proven successful in searching and destroying enemy elements that used the highways after dark. The gunship and OH-6 had no idea we were in the area, so we sprawled in the mud and held our breath as they drew closer. We were only thirty or forty yards off the highway and would be easy prey for this deadly team. Since we had left our rucksacks and helmets back at the bridge and wore flop hats and camo grease, we might easily be mistaken for a platoon of VC prowling the night.

We lay petrified and watched as the choppers drew closer. I thought that if I closed my eyes everything might be all right, but fear told me we would be no match for the horrid miniguns of the Cobra. If those searchlights picked us up, it would be a matter of two or three seconds before the miniguns vomited out hundreds of rounds per second and ground us into the mud and rice plants. Someone asked Lieutenant Hernandez if we ought to try to shoot out the floodlights, but that would have meant sudden death, since the Cobra pilot was trained to fire instantly at muzzle flashes. The lights reached the far edge of the rice field we were hiding in. It was only a matter of seconds before the choppers would be over us, and we were frozen like fallen statues as we waited for the inevitable. The OH-6 was just reaching us when it suddenly swung its searchlights away and danced them over the fields on the opposite side of the road. We lay motionless as the two choppers lumbered past us and moved on down the highway. In a couple of minutes they were gone. We stood up in the darkness and quietly joked with each other about how scared we all had been. Call it fate, luck, or whatever, but I'll always believe that God answered my prayer, and probably the prayers of several others.

We proceeded on our mission, only to find a village full of women and children. They had probably been warned of our approach and managed to send off any VC soldiers who may have been in the area. We stayed out most of the night, later settling down in a thickly wooded area to pull a couple of hours of guard and wait till morning before returning to An Lo Bridge.

Back at the bridge, we were told to retire to the bunkers and get some much-needed sleep. We later woke to shouts of excitement. I crawled from the foul-smelling bunker and squinted my eyes at something we had not seen in many weeks—sunshine. The monsoon season was finally coming to an end, and we stood in small groups and laughed out loud at how good the warm sun felt on our bodies.

Later that day a supply truck arrived from LZ Jane and brought enough rations and supplies to carry us through the next few days. Riding in the back of that truck was Tan Lo, our Vietnamese scout, whom we had not seen since departing Cu Chi. He had been brought north to rejoin us and serve as our scout and interpreter. He was smiling like a little kid when several of us walked over to greet him. He proceeded to tell us of the fighting going on down south and of the problems he had had in trying to reach us in our new area of operation. He was a good soldier and dedicated to his country, but his career was about to come to an abrupt end. He talked with us for a few minutes and then walked away to find our CO and inform him that he was back and anxious to serve Alpha Company. As he walked past a small group of GIs from the 1st Platoon, his rifle accidentally discharged and sent a single round into the soldiers a few feet away. I turned to see who had fired a shot and saw the soldiers scatter like a covey of quail—all, that is, except one. A young Latin soldier lay motionless as Tan Lo and others raced over to see if he was all right. Someone shouted for a medic, and I ran over to see if I could help. The young soldier, who had recently joined us as a replacement, lay stone dead from an M16 round through his heart. Tan Lo stood there with a look of shock and disbelief on his face and began to jabber in Vietnamese instead of English. There was nothing we could do for either of this tragedy's victims, and I felt sorry for the tall, skinny Vietnamese soldier as the first sergeant took his rifle from him and led him away for his own safety until the MPs could arrive.

The next morning we packed our gear and waited on Charlie Company to move in and take our place at the bridge. When they arrived, we saddled up and moved down Highway One to a long, straight stretch to wait for choppers to come in and pick us up. We were told that we would fly several miles south toward Hue to help start a new base camp for the 2nd Brigade. We would be there for only three days, so we knew our time would be spent building bunkers and stringing wire. We geared ourselves for hard, boring work, but our spirits were somewhat lifted since we would be working in warm sunshine instead of the menacing rain and mud.

CHAPTER FOUR

LZ SALLY

The hot, bright sun was a welcome sight after the weeks of misery we had grown accustomed to, and it quickly baked the dark, fertile mud into hard, dusty clay. Building Landing Zone Sally was a relief from working in the villages, since it allowed us to spend a few days in the security of a base camp, and it also gave our feet a break. Jungle rot plagued all of us—over the last month or two water and mud had been slowly dissolving our feet. Eight of my toenails had fallen off, yet my feet were in relatively good shape compared to some. Roger Clapeckni was hobbling around on feet that had deep, bleeding cracks around and between his toes. Most of us went barefoot or in our sock feet as we dug the new perimeter bunkers and strung the concertina wire. Sally was to be a large, sprawling camp that would be home to the 2nd Brigade. It was located on gently rolling grasslands in the shadows of a nearby mountain range. It quickly grew from infancy to adolescence as sectors of the vast perimeter were linked together, and a short dirt runway for small aircraft was scratched out in its center. Tents were erected, chopper pads laid, latrines and showers constructed, artillery pieces flown in, and necessary work areas put into operation as this olive-drab minicity grew into a functional service center for the many hundreds of line doggies it would support.

We stayed at LZ Sally for four days and had just completed the perimeter defenses when we learned we would soon be leaving for a new AO, one we were somewhat leery of—the mountains. We had not worked in the mountains and were more afraid of the unknown than of the giant, jungle-covered peaks themselves. They were beautiful and stately as they stood silently over the vast deltas of rice fields and small villages. We would soon find out that the North Vietnamese walked as freely among these giants as they did in downtown Hanoi. It would be our job to seek them out and make contact, to keep them on the defensive rather than the offensive.

On the morn of our fourth day at Sally, we left via the rear gate, which led to a huge garbage hole dug by bulldozers. As our column wound its way past the fly-infested sump, small boys who had been picking through the trash came over and begged us for smokes or C rations. We joked with them and relinquished a few cigarettes and sticks of gum. In return we received a quick grin and an acknowledgment that we were "numba one." We progressed slowly toward the mountains, searching small hamlets and single hootches on our way. At one lonely farm site we found an ancient-looking man taking care of a small boy. It puzzled us, since the two of them appeared to be much poorer than the average peasants and no one was around to take care of them. They gladly accepted a few cans of C rats, and in gratitude the old man offered us the only thing he had—a drink of hot, dirty-looking tea, which was brewing over an open fire. Bud and I accepted, looking at each other with an uncertain glance, for we knew we would pay for this gesture of friendship with stomach cramps and diarrhea. We pretended to sip from the dirty glasses, and then wandering off behind the hootch, we quietly pitched the yellow liquid into a bamboo thicket.

Moving on toward the foothills, we stopped among several huge bomb craters, the results of a B52 strike. We were to take a short break, so Scotty, Ric, and I crawled over the edge of a large, water-filled crater and settled down for a quick cigarette. We were enjoying the shade from the semijungle growth when Scotty quietly motioned for us to be still; he clicked the safety off his rifle and lifted it in the direction of a nearby thicket. Ric and I crouched lower in the crater and brought our rifles over the edge, trying to figure out what Scotty was peering at. I whispered, "What's wrong?" and he replied, "Don't move! I see movement in the thicket, and it's not one of us." I squinted in the bright sun to see if I could pick up the outline of an enemy soldier, but could see nothing. Then a small tree moved slightly and bent to the ground as a giant snake slid slowly from an overhanging limb. It was the biggest snake I'd ever seen, and we watched in amazement as its huge body quietly glided through the bushes. It was big, brown, and ugly, and we were glad when the word was passed along to "pick up and move out." The three of us told our story to anyone who would listen, but no one would believe the monstrous size of the reptile.

We made our way into the mountains and discovered endless, well-beaten paths beneath the triple canopy of jungle growth. We tried cutting our way through the thick undergrowth in order to avoid the trails, but the going was so tough we decided to stick to the trails and take our chances on walking head-on into an element of North Vietnamese, or triggering land mines or booby traps. Our point men worked slowly and methodically as they led us around the mountains and deeper and deeper into dangerous territory.

The jungle was pleasantly cool, and a bounty of crystal-clear water poured from the mountainsides. It wasn't long before we discovered a menacing little creature that was everywhere and totally unavoidable. The vines and shrubs were covered with small, black land leeches. They attached themselves to our skin or clothing as we brushed against the foliage, and most of us were covered with these slimy little creatures before we even knew they were around. If we snatched them off quickly, in disgust, we bled profusely from the small, round holes that had been gnawed in our skin. These land leeches were only about an inch long, but were just as revolting as their six-inch-long cousins, which swam in the paddies and canals of Vietnam. We had humped past the first range of hills and had stopped for a rest and quick meal when Ken Fryer suddenly yelled out for a medic. We thought he had impaled himself on a punji stake, but found out that he had stepped behind a tree to urinate and discovered a leech on the tip of the most private part of his body. He was embarrassed beyond words and repeatedly asked Doc Reems, "What are you going to do?" as Doc surveyed the situation. The whole platoon broke out in loud laughter as word of Ken's predicament quickly spread. A crowd gathered to watch and tease as Doc prepared to loosen the hold of the tiny creature on this muscular, black soldier. I could have sworn I detected a blush on Ken's sweaty face as he stood with his pants around his ankles while Doc dabbed the leach with a cotton swab soaked in mosquito lotion. The incident had briefly taken our minds off the danger surrounding us, but our attention was abruptly snapped back into place by the far-off chatter of machine guns.

We turned our heads toward the distant firing, which was coming from above us. At the peak of a nearby mountain, a Huey soared in circles like a vulture, allowing its gunners to fire directly at the mountaintop. The action was at least a mile away, and we could not see what the chopper was firing at. Another suddenly appeared and took up the same course of action. Together they circled the peak for ten minutes until one finally landed on the grassy top while the other continued to fly close by. As we watched, someone jumped from the chopper and ran around picking up small objects. Then as quickly as they had come, they departed. Our curiosity was getting the best of us when the CO radioed our platoon leaders to advise that the choppers had just annihilated a heavy mortar platoon on the mountain. We were ordered to hike to the peak the following morning and investigate.

Early the next day we found out that walking the trails that meandered through the valleys was a lot easier than climbing the peaks with a full pack and rifle. We finally reached the top and found the results of what must have been a turkey shoot for the two choppers the day before. Sprawled in the open were twenty-five or thirty dead North Vietnamese who had been slaughtered by the door-gunners on the circling Hueys. Some were caught in half-constructed bunkers; others had tried to hide in the sparse brush dotting the mountaintop. They had met a quick and savage death, and their horrified expressions reflected the terror that rained down on them from the sky. Most of their small weapons were gone, which explained what the individual from the chopper had raced around and gathered up. The only weapons remaining were two 82mm mortar tubes and one 61mm mortar with base plates and plenty of ammunition. We searched the mutilated bodies and took Chi-Com grenades from them. Playfully we threw them down the steep slopes and watched them explode far below us. On one young soldier's body I found a letter. On the envelope was a North Vietnamese stamp depicting an American bomber being shot down by communist gunners—a strange form of propaganda! I wondered what message the letter held.

We descended from the mountain and rendezvoused with a chopper that delivered to us our new platoon sergeant. His name was Staff Sergeant Sneeds. His easygoing personality and businesslike manner quickly told us we would like him, but he could never take the place of Sfc. Eddie Hands. We all remembered the promise Sergeant Hands had made about his return, so we knew we wouldn't let anyone permanently fill his boots.

That night each platoon went separate ways to set up an ambush.

Ours was at the junction of two well-used trails. The ambush sight was a steep slope overlooking the trails. To prevent us from sliding into the kill zone as we slept, we ended up tying ourselves to trees with our belts. The night was uneventful except for a torrential rainstorm that nearly washed us off the mountainside. Although the storm was over quickly, it left us wet and miserable for the rest of the night.

We spent two more days combing the complex network of trails, finding more signs of the enemy—footprints, spent Russian ammunition cartridges. Jerald LeDeux from Louisiana was walking point for our platoon one afternoon and walked head-on into two NVA soldiers with their weapons slung over their shoulders. The trail we were walking made a sharp turn and the three of them had managed to reach the turn at the same instant; Jerald said he could have reached out and shaken hands with one of them. He was so surprised that he emptied a full magazine at them and amazingly did not hit either one. One of the NVA dropped an RPG rocket launcher in his flight—at least Jerald knew this was one weapon that could not be used against us.

We had worked our way closer to the Laotian border, and that night we lay in the wet, black jungle and listened to the sound of engines rumbling in the distance. Our only guess was that Uncle Ho's troops were trucking fresh supplies down the infamous Ho Chi Minh Trail, supplies that would soon be thrown against the massive American buildup in the I Corps area. Later in the night we were aroused by what sounded like distant thunder, but the yellow flashes from the far side of the next ridge told us that a sortie of B52s was unloading its deadly cargo on the convoys we had heard earlier. We could feel the earth convulse, then a thundering roll of explosions as the giant bombs gouged out craters along the hidden highways. The swept-wing bombers were so high we could not even hear them, and I lay there in the dark and wondered how impersonal the war must be for those men soaring more than 50,000 feet above us in their star-littered battlefield.

The next day found Alpha Company split into three elements as each platoon went its separate way in search of the enemy. The 3rd Platoon was slowly winding its way down steep trails that would lead eventually to the Song Bo River. Our squad was in the lead, and Scotty and I were walking point together some thirty or forty yards in front of the rest of the platoon. We worked well together and had developed a language of hand signals and body movements—silence had to be maintained while scouting the trails. Our rifles were always held at the ready with safeties switched off so as to have an advantage over the slack NVA soldiers who usually walked with weapons slung over their shoulders.

The sun was high and was turning the jungle into a steam bath as we picked our way along the rocky trail. A sharp turn in the trail suddenly left us staring into the mouth of a large bunker only a few yards ahead. Instinctively we threw ourselves into the brush on either side of the trail; we expected to receive machine-gun fire, but moments went by without any defensive action from the well-hidden fighting position. Scotty and I glanced at each other across the path and motioned that one of us needed to race back and warn the rest of the platoon as it slowly advanced toward us along the winding trail. Scotty signaled that he would stay in position while I returned to inform Lieutenant Hernandez of our predicament. Sweat from the tension was dripping from my face as I sped quietly back up the trail. I soon reached the head of the column and whispered the news to Lieutenant Hernandez. After we quickly discussed the situation, he radioed our FO for possible artillery support from LZ Sally.

His next order sent a cold chill down my spine. He ordered me to return to Scotty and the two of us to move on and search the area. I was horrified at what might lie ahead, but understood that it was necessary to scout out the potential danger zone before leading the entire platoon into a possible ambush. My heart raced with fear as I returned to where Scotty lay in the brush and whispered to him what our mission now was. His expression also reflected a fear gnawing at his insides, but he nodded in agreement and crawled out on the path beside me. He stood up, and with slow, deliberate steps, we moved forward and searched the bunker. We then moved on down the trail, where we discovered more fresh footprints and a few scattered cigarette butts. With nerves as taut as bowstrings, we crept forward, not making a sound, and suddenly found ourselves standing at the end of the trail as it opened up into a uniquely constructed complex of bunkers, hootches, and ammo caches. The highly functional base camp was as large as a football field and was completely hidden from scouting aircraft by a thick canopy of tall jungle trees. We crouched beside a large tree and surveyed the area before going any farther. It looked deserted, but past experience warned us that enemy gunners might let us advance and lead more troops into the open before cutting us down. We strained our eyes and ears, trying to detect any signs of life, but only the jungle birds could be heard as they screamed out the message of our presence.

A moment away from the war: chapel services, held in the courtyard of a Buddhist shrine. The chaplains tried to visit each unit in the boonies at least once a month.

Author's friend Bud Dykes with a captured AK-47 at LZ Jane. Alpha Company helped build this small firebase near Hai Lang.

Children begging for gum and candy. The boy on the right is smoking a ciga- rette.

Young girls carrying loads of over one- hundred pounds on their shoulders. Next to them on the path is a "spider hole"— underground fighting positions built by the VC and NVA.

Jeep after taking a direct hit from a 122mm rocket at LZ Jane.

Alpha Company moves to the mountains overlooking LZ Sally. In the foreground is a bomb crater from a B-52 air raid.

Line doggie sitting next to a "spider hole." These holes were practically indestructible and almost impossible to detect until you were on top of them.

South Vietnamese soldier questions a captured VC. After being threatened with a knife, the prisoner told everything he knew.

The author moved into this "apartment" after the battle of Phuoc Yen.

Hueys come in to transport Alpha Company to a raging firefight.

Heliborne assault into Eight Klick Ville. Note the C-ration can ingeniously attached to the machine gun, to feed ammo belts smoothly into the gun.

Alpha Company, pinned down just outside of Eight Klick Ville, watches an F-4 Phantom drop bombs on the dug-in enemy. At this canal one of Alpha Company's troopers had his eyes shot out by an NVA sniper.

A buffalo boy followed the author's unit during the day. They later discovered that each evening the boy would report their location to the VC.

Perimeter bunker armed with a 50-caliber machine gun protects the troops at "Coco Beach," an R & R base on the Gulf of Tonkin.

Footbridge over a stream in Eight Klick Ville. These bridges were constructed by the Viet Cong and often boobytrapped.

The snow-white sands of Firebase 'Sandy, which the Third Herd helped build into the shape of a star. The Screaming Eagles were supported from this firebase with artillery and supply choppers.

We stood and slowly began to move into the open. As we advanced toward the center of the camp, we split up and checked the scattered hootches and bunkers to our front. The sector I was searching sloped downhill to the banks of the Song Bo River, and before I knew what had happened, Scotty and I had moved out of sight of each other. I stood alone, petrified, in the center of that enemy camp, wrestling desperately with my fear as it threatened to shatter my concentration. I turned to where I thought Scotty should be and managed to whistle like a bird in order to get his attention. There was no answer, so I whistled again and listened intently for his returning signal. With great relief, I detected a faint whistle. He had moved over a small hill to search out a complex of bunkers and ammo dumps. In the excitement, he also had not realized we had become separated. As we met at the top of the small hill, a slight grin from Scotty told me he had been as frightened as I and was as relieved to see my sweaty face as I was to see his. We knelt to brief each other and concluded that the camp had been abandoned earlier that morning. A faint wisp of smoke from a recent fire next to stacked cooking utensils suggested that this was merely a supply camp and had been manned by a small element of North Vietnamese soldiers. They evidently had stationed guards on the nearby trails and had taken flight as our platoon approached.

The discovery was exciting, the catch was enormous, and to the victor belonged the spoils. Scotty and I were elated and could hardly wait to tell the rest of the platoon. This time I stayed at the camp while he went back for the others. Although I was still scared about being alone, excitement about the find soon displaced my fear.

When the rest of the platoon arrived, we designated several men as security and others as search elements. Lieutenant Hernandez radioed the CO about our find, but he was with another platoon, and it would take several hours before the rest of the company humped over the mountains and valleys separating us.

We were amazed at how ingenious our enemy was proving to be. They had built a dock, which extended about twelve feet from the riverbank and was about a foot below the surface of the water. Supplies were brought downriver at night and unloaded on this underwater dock, which could not be detected from the air. They had also built a mess hootch for preparing meals. It was partially dug out of a steep bank and covered with a thatched roof; the fireplace was dug into the bank and a long trench extended from the top of the fireplace eighty or ninety feet up the slope. The trench was covered by a thick layer of palm fronds and leaves, which filtered the smoke so a telltale column would not rise straight up through the treetops and give away their location. Another trick was stuffing mortar shells and RPG rockets down the center of bamboo thickets. The bamboo in the jungles was big and lush and grew in clumps of fifty to sixty separate stalks. The NVA soldiers would shove the projectiles, many still wrapped in plastic, as deep as they could into the clumps of bamboo, protecting them from artillery shrapnel and the damp earth. We also found one cluster stuffed full of brand-new Russian AK47 rifles still covered in packing grease.

By midafternoon the rest of Alpha Company had joined us, and we continued to pile up tons of weapons and munitions. According to an article published much later in an army newspaper, the following supplies were taken from this well-hidden North Vietnamese camp: 330 RPG rockets, 38 122mm rockets with 16 warheads, 18 new AK47 rifles, 321 rounds of 60mm mortar shells, 170 rounds of 82mm mortar shells, 24,000 rounds of Russian 7.62mm rifle ammunition, 28 cases of high explosives, 2,800 nonelectric blasting caps, more than 2,000 pounds of other assorted munitions, field radios, medical supplies, and a complete field mess kitchen. It was estimated that these supplies were part of those used on the siege of Hue during the Tet Offensive, and one could only guess how long this base had been used to bring in goods and redistribute them to NVA and VC elements in the area.

Our next task was to extract the supplies from their jungle hideaway and ship them back to LZ Sally. Attempts to load the bulky war goods onto choppers hovering over the river were fruitless due to the deep water and swift current—we spilled more in the dirty, brown river than we loaded onto the choppers. After floundering about in the river with arm loads of the heavy munitions, this effort was soon abandoned. We decided that the only way to load the Hueys was to cut out a landing zone near the riverbank. Axes and machetes were flown in, and we immediately set about clearing the area.

A near-level spot close to the riverbank was selected, and we began chopping and hacking at the thick growth and large trees. Other work parties gathered up the limbs and tree trunks and rolled them into the river. After nearly a day, our landing zone was completed. We gathered the massive stacks of supplies and piled them near the clearing.

News of our discovery had spread through the nearby base camps, and we learned that the commanding general of the 101st Airborne

Division was flying out to have a personal look. Most of us dreaded the thought of his visit—it meant we had to act like garrison troops instead of the seasoned combat soldiers we really were. The first ridiculous order was for us to remove all rounds from our rifle chambers, look alert, and disperse into small groups for safety reasons. We would go through the motions and act as though we were back at Fort Campbell when we all knew as soon as the general departed we would chamber a round in our rifles and go about our duties of soldiering. Another order to "look alert" brought a laugh from us, and we made a game out of practicing alert poses.

The general's highly waxed Huey soon flew in, accompanied by two Cobra gunships circling nearby. A slight man of small frame, he looked like a toy soldier as he stepped from his chopper wearing starched fatigues and spit-shined jungle boots. Our CO raced forward to greet him, self-consciously positioning himself so the general wouldn't notice the large rip in the seat of his pants. Most of us had stopped wearing underwear due to the constant plague of diarrhea, and we tried not to laugh at the snow-white patch of ass glistening through the tear in the captain's britches.

The general must have asked who had discovered the enemy camp, because our CO pointed toward us, and the two of them started in our direction. The general came over and spoke with Scotty, Lieutenant Hernandez, and me as he browsed among the stacks of weapons. A small group of general's aides—lieutenants, captains, and a major— followed him around in their immaculate uniforms, watching every move as though they were afraid he was going to step in something. He continued to ask questions, some of them absolutely meaningless: "Where are you from in the States?" "Have you been on R & R yet?" After a few more minutes he told us, "You're doing a good job. Keep up the good work." The general obviously had no understanding of the life of a line doggie. His departing remark was, "You troops are the dirtiest and most unkempt looking soldiers that I've seen lately!" The general really did a lot for morale. Our CO turned red and stuttered in response that he would make sure we shaved and cleaned up as soon as possible. He almost had a fit when he noticed several of us giving the finger to the general as his chopper lifted off and turned down the river.

The next two days found us still at the supply base loading chopper after chopper with enemy weapons. Ric Ricart had come down with a severe intestinal disorder and was tagged by our medics to be sent back to LZ Sally for further treatment. Medevacs were not used for such minor cases, so he would have to wait to fly back on one of the Hueys hauling out enemy supplies. When the next slick flew in and settled on the small riverside landing zone, we loaded it with cases of the munitions, leaving a small hole for Ric to squeeze into. We signaled the pilot to take off, and the big bird groaned and strained to lift its heavy load into the hot jungle air. We had evidently loaded the bird with too much weight, since it climbed to about ten or fifteen feet and could go no higher. The Huey began to slowly descend tail first toward the river. We watched in horror, with the wash from the straining rotor blades blowing dirt and debris into our eyes. I was sure the aircraft was doomed, but quick action prevented a tragedy. One of the door-gunners sprang from his seat and climbed onto the pile of supplies that filled the craft. Placing his boot in the center of Ric's back, he sharply kicked him out of the chopper. He then shoved out several cases of munitions, and the chopper began to level off and climb. The pilot radioed that he would take the partial load back to LZ Sally and return for his passenger.

We raced over to where Ric lay in the brush. He had landed hard and was trying to get on his feet while throwing up all over himself. Except for a few bruises, he was unhurt. He mumbled that he understood the gunner had done what was necessary to prevent the chopper from crashing and probably causing several fatalities. Ric's buddies helped him down to the river, where he walked in up to his chest and washed the vomit from his clothes. The Huey soon returned and took Ric and a smaller load of supplies back to Sally.

After completing our chores at the enemy base camp, Sgt. "Pat" Patterson of the 2nd Platoon took charge of rigging all the bunkers and hootches with plastic explosives. Some of the bunkers were massive, and Sergeant Pat loaded them with several cases of C-4. Time-delayed fuses were used to give us plenty of time to depart the area before the charges detonated. Sergeant Pat stayed back with one of his squads to make sure all fuses were burning properly; we humped to the top of a nearby mountain and held up to wait for the trailing element. By radio contact we knew they had lit the fuses and were on their way. Several minutes passed as we rested and enjoyed a cigarette. Then a tremendous explosion shook the jungle for miles around and a small, mushroom-shaped cloud of dust and smoke rose from the valley below us—they had done their job well.

We stayed in the mountains for a few more days and engaged in a small firefight with a squad-size element of NVA. They had been spotted trying to escape over a small hill. Though we outnumbered them ten to one, they took a defensive stand and fought back when we opened up on them. Two of the North Vietnamese were killed, and the others escaped to fight us another day.

Figuring that the enemy had moved out of the area due to our presence, battalion headquarters ordered us back to LZ Sally. It took us nearly a day to make the long trek back to base camp, but we welcomed the walk, even in the stifling heat. We were all anxious to leave the dangerous mountains.

LZ Sally had grown into a small city while we were gone, and it felt good to be able to relax within the perimeter. After being assigned to perimeter bunkers, we were instructed not to get too comfortable because we would be going back to An Lo Bridge the next day. It was still a relief to be able to let our guard down and pass the time with our buddies over a warm can of beer and a deck of cards.

Mail bags that had been collecting for the past two or three days were brought around. Joey Miller had received a large package that excited all of us—his mom had mailed him a case of Coca-Cola. Joey called all of us over to share his prize. He opened the well-sealed case, took out a shiny red can, and pulled the tab. Instead of the familiar "phssst" it gave out a dull "clink" that brought a look of uncertainty to his face. Slowly he turned up the can to his lips and poured the liquid down his throat. As we anxiously waited for his approval to open more cans of the delicious treat he was so unselfishly sharing with us, Joey pulled the can from his mouth and uttered one word—"Water!"

We couldn't believe what we had heard. How could a can of Coke taste like water? The explanation was simple. Fishing around in the discarded case, he found a note from his mom, folded and stuffed inside. Concerned about her son's casual statements in his letters about the foul-tasting water we had to drink, she had visited a local bottling company and talked them into canning a case of water for her son in Vietnam. We were all let down, but we savored the cool, clean liquid and pretended it was Coke.

The next morning Bravo Company moved in to take our positions of perimeter guard, and we packed up our meager belongings and boarded two-and-a-half-ton trucks to leave for An Lo Bridge. As the trucks lumbered into the compound surrounding the bridge, we were greeted by the small children we had made friends with on our previous visit.

Perimeter sectors were assigned, and we moved to our positions to set up for a four- or five-day stay.

The stench and filth had increased in wholesale quantities since we had been here. The most noticeable problem was the millions of flies inhabiting the small camp. We soon made a game out of betting on how many flies would crawl into a napping GI's mouth before he woke and brushed them away. Decomposing bodies drifted down the river with the current, and once, while bathing in the river, a soldier was embraced by the outstretched arms of a dead North Vietnamese. The body bobbed beneath the bridge and continued toward the sea.

Our second day at An Lo Bridge, I became seriously ill with a stomach disorder. Doubled over with cramps, I walked down into a garbage sump, where I suffered extreme diarrhea and vomiting at the same time. Doc Richardson helped me out of the trash sump and told me he was sending me back to LZ Sally for treatment. Curled up in the fetal position, I lay on the hot steel floor of a three-quarter-ton truck as it crashed into every pothole on Highway One. We finally arrived back at Sally, and I made my way over to the med tent. A cupful of thick, chalky liquid brought some relief to my misery. I slowly regained my strength and after three days felt well enough to return to the company. Ric Ricart, still at base camp following his episode of being kicked out of the chopper, and I would go back together. Alpha Company had just left An Lo Bridge so we would fly out to join them on the next day's log ship. On this last night at base camp we decided to conduct a recon patrol on the mess tent and try to find a small prize of something good to eat to take back to our buddies in the fields.

Ric and I waited till around midnight so we could sneak into the mess tent with as little chance of detection as possible. We crawled the last few yards through the black shadows of nearby supply tents and hootches. Our destination finally reached, we sat quietly in the shadows to catch our breath. We weren't sure whether any of the cooks slept in the mess tent, so we entered slowly and lit a match after closing the door flap.

Before us in the dim light of the flickering flame lay enough food to feed an army—literally. Tables were covered with dozens of loaves of freshly baked bread and stacks of canned goods. Refrigerator units were bulging with fruit, milk, and large, juicy roasts cooked that afternoon. We both tucked our shirts into our pants and quickly decided what items we could "borrow" for our buddies. Ric filled his shirt while I held a match, and then it was my turn. I stuffed two roasts into my shirt and grabbed two loaves of bread along with a half-gallon can of some unknown substance. Noises outside made us cut short our recon mission, so we crawled under the rear wall of the tent and escaped with the loot.

The next day we returned to the fields with our rucksacks loaded with the food we were eager to share with our friends. The roasts and bread were sliced with machetes and made into sandwiches. I left the can in my pack, since it turned out to be cooking cherries instead of the peanut butter I had hoped for.

I carried those cherries in my rucksack for a couple of days until the extra weight became a nuisance. During a break from the afternoon heat, I decided to open them and pass the can around, but they were yellow, and extremely sweet, so no one wanted any. I decided not to waste my efforts, and ate as much of the sweet fruit as I could hold. Within two hours I knew I had made a mistake. My recent sickness returned, and cramps and nausea overtook me. We had set up a company perimeter in a large graveyard, and I lay quietly in the tall grass and vomited up the cherries. My body was racked with chills and my temperature soared to 105 degrees. I remember Doc Reems tying a medical tag to my shirt as he called for a medevac chopper.

In a semiconscious state I barely remember the chopper ride to the 22nd Surgical Hospital in Phu Bai. As I was being carried in for admittance I heard one of the medics mention malaria as he read the casualty tag Doc had tied to my shirt. Several medics cut off my clothes and boots; I tried my best not to vomit on them. Immediate action was taken to lower my temperature: They lifted me onto a rubber cot, strapped down my arms and legs, and covered me completely with bucketfuls of crushed ice.

A doctor soon arrived and talked to me about malaria, mentioning several tests that would have to be administered before their suspicions were confirmed. After a day and a half of tests, the same doctor returned and informed me they had diagnosed my illness as "intestinal parasites." He laughed at the puzzled look on my face and then proceeded to tell me I had an acute case of "worms." I couldn't believe what I heard and asked him how I could have contracted such a thing. He answered, "Drinking dirty water, eating native food, or sleeping on the ground where parasite eggs could have entered your bloodstream through a scratch." I qualified for all of these. He assured me that this was a common thing among foot soldiers and easily taken care of.

I was then flown to the 9th Field Hospital in Nha Trang, where they stuffed me full of jellylike pills that looked and smelled like those I used to give my hunting dogs back in North Carolina. I spent about a week in the hospital, thoroughly enjoying the cleanliness and relaxation. Going to the hospital was just like a vacation to a line doggie—the food was good, there were real beds to sleep in, clean toilet facilities, showers, and all of the other trivial conveniences that an infantryman had learned to do without. I lay in that hospital bed thinking about how easy it was as an American to ignore the comforts of life until they were no longer available.

Although it was delightful to be able to sleep all night and have the privilege of being waited on by the efficient hospital staff, I soon learned that a stay in the hospital caused mental anguish for most line doggies. If wounds or illnesses were not extremely serious, the grunts were patched up and sent back to their units as soon as possible. But even a brief hospital stay was mental torture: while lying in bed they had time to reflect on the situation and realize just how scared they were about returning to combat. A soldier doesn't have much time in the fields to think of his fear, but when he is removed from combat conditions, his mind can play tricks on him, turning his dreams at night and his thoughts in the day into horrible nightmares. We heard rumors about line doggies who had cut their wrists, taken overdoses, or even drunk from the same glass as a hepatitis patient in order to keep from being sent back to "the line." I experienced these feelings myself and constantly fought my fears as my hospital stay drew to a close.

Some thirty pounds thinner, I returned to LZ Sally by hitchhiking on C-130s and supply trucks. After a day and a half at the dusty base camp, I readied my equipment and drew a new rifle for my return to the fields. I flew out to Quang Dien on the next day's log ship and joined the company in the middle of a nearly destroyed village, deserted and overgrown with lush vegetation. Staff Sergeant Sneed informed me that the enemy was everywhere and they had already engaged in several small skirmishes and sniper attacks. The next day proved this information to be true, as we walked head-on into a company of North Vietnamese.

The 1st Platoon received the inital attack—heavy machine guns and mortars ripped into their flank. One of the men was killed instantly when a mortar round exploded beside him and tore off most of his head. Two more from the 1st Platoon had nearly every bone in their legs crushed by concentrated fire from a heavy machine gun. The 2nd Platoon was trying to work its way around the right flank of the enemy positions, but were pinned down by deadly accurate mortar fire that crashed into them at a rate of about one round every ten seconds.

Lieutenant Hernandez was screaming out orders for us to advance to a nearby hedgerow, but we were held up by two enemy soldiers in separate spider holes. They had evidently rehearsed their defensive actions, because every time one paused to reload, the other would hold us down with blistering fire from his AK47. The cross fire had us pinned behind an old house only partially standing. We pressed our bodies into the rubble while the enemy slugs sought us out from less than fifty feet away. Sergeant Tom Moore had managed to crawl near one of the enemy positions, and he shouted for us to give him covering fire as he jumped to his feet and charged the position, spraying the small bunker with his M16. His gallant effort resulted in the death of the North Vietnamese, but as Tom turned to race back to cover, the other enemy soldier shot him in the back with a short burst from his AK.

Tom fell in a quivering heap. As he tried to climb to his feet, his legs buckled beneath him. The enemy gunner then fired point-blank into his body and took the remaining few ounces of life. Roy Hill was nearer to Tom than any of us, and when he saw his friend being slaughtered, he jumped to his feet to race out and drag him back to safety. The North Vietnamese soldier opened up on Roy, hitting him in the ear with a single round. Roy fell hard, blood gushing from the hole in his head. There was a slight pause as we all froze for a moment to stare at the bodies of our two downed comrades. It must have been anger that welled within us, for we all rose to our knees and sprayed the area with our rifles. The enemy soldier ceased his firing. Bud Dykes yelled for cover and raced toward the bunker with a grenade clutched in his hand. He hurled the grenade into the bunker and cursed the enemy soldier as he turned to race away. Bud was not quick enough—the tough little enemy pitched the grenade back at him and it landed at his heels. It exploded viciously as Bud tried to throw his body over a pile of rubble. The concussion rolled him into a trench, where he lay stunned and wounded, with searing shrapnel wounds in his thighs and knees.

The enemy seemed indestructible. He had managed to take down three of us, and we still could not maneuver on his position without being fired upon. The final chapter was written for this fierce fighter when one of our "cherries" crawled forward with a LAW (light anti-tank weapon). We gave him cover as he readied the rocket launcher and took careful aim at the enemy bunker. The launcher belched out flame and smoke as the rocket sped for its target. The resulting explosion tore off the top of the enemy bunker and decapitated its occupant.

We raced forward to attend to our fallen comrades and knew instantly that Tom Moore was dead. A glaze had already settled over his eyes. To our relief, Roy Hill was alive. His head wound was still spurting blood. We carefully rolled him over and Doc Reems began to check his wound. It was a miracle—Roy came to and started to get up. We held him down while Doc checked his head and discovered that the bullet had merely gone through the fleshy lobe of his ear and glanced off the thick portion of skull under it. Bud was limping around with a bad shrapnel wound from his own grenade: a large chunk of steel had buried itself deep in the back of his knee. He nearly passed out from the pain as Doc wrapped his leg. We quickly assigned men to carry Tom's body and help the wounded back to a dust-off location. We then proceeded on to assist the rest of the company as the fierce battle continued to our front.

By the time we reached the company, 155mm artillery shells were pulverizing the enemy positions. There was a lull in the ground fighting while we watched whole trees and hootches being shredded into small pieces and thrown skyward, with acrid smoke and dust billowing from the explosions.

A FAC (forward air control) plane buzzed our position, and we threw yellow and purple smoke grenades to identify our lines to the lone pilot who flew within rifle range of the enemy soldiers. I always enjoyed watching those brave pilots buzzing their small-engine craft just above the trees. Their mission was lonely and dangerous as they coordinated the infantry and the jet pilots who screamed through the skies to deliver payloads of deadly ordnance. The FAC planes were unarmed except for a half-dozen smoke rockets that the pilot used to mark targets for the fighter-bombers. One of the FAC pilots had a pronounced Southern drawl. He and his cohorts used a language all their own as they conversed between us on the ground and the jets circling in the sky. This particular pilot always concluded his mission by drawling out, "Y'all have a nice day, now heah!" just before signing off and flying back to home base.

The jets and artillery pieces pounded the enemy for the rest of the afternoon. Just before dark we moved in to clean up any resistance that remained. We tangled with small elements of the enemy, but they were so disoriented and stunned from the barrage of bombs and artillery shells that we were able to quickly neutralize them as we moved through the flattened village. We found total destruction and carnage. The North Vietnamese evidently had not had time to dig in as they normally did. The spider holes and shallow trenches provided no protection from the hammering they received. Dismembered and charred bodies lay everywhere, along with the twisted remains of their weapons. They had suffered heavy losses: we counted at least seventy bodies strewn about the small village.

The next day we continued our search-and-destroy mission through the deserted villages. They had long since been left to the VC and NVA, and the trails and small family plots had begun to grow over with weeds and vines. We made no contact that day, but found three more dead NVA who had managed to flee a short distance from the previous day's battle, only to collapse and die from their wounds during the night.

Darkness found us setting up a company perimeter in a large graveyard. Lieutenant Hernandez approached me with orders to take out an LP approximately 200 yards from the perimeter. I chose Buddy Travino and Larry Young. The three of us waited together near the perimeter for total darkness to conceal our movement. We covered ourselves with mosquito lotion and piled our rucksacks and helmets near the CP. Carrying only rifles and grenades, we checked with each position on our sector of the perimeter and informed them of the general direction we were heading. Movement was slow through the overgrown trails, and we took our time in the dark, praying we wouldn't trigger a booby trap or walk into an element of enemy soldiers. It took us nearly an hour to reach our destination. Even then we weren't sure we were in the right spot, because the sky was cloud-covered and the night jet black.

We stumbled onto the remains of an old concrete-block house and decided to hide among the rubble, which would provide cover in case we were attacked. Without a sound the three of us picked out a small place to settle down, quietly moving aside chunks of concrete so we could lay low in the thick grass. Only a few words were whispered as Buddy and I lay down to get some sleep while Larry pulled the first watch. Not more than an hour had gone by when I woke up in fright— my right leg felt as though it was on fire. My first thought was that I had bedded down with a deadly bamboo viper or that a spider had bitten me on the thigh. I sat up to gather my thoughts and detected a faint odor of lighter fluid. Reaching inside the large kangaroo pocket on my pant leg, I pulled out the small can of lighter fluid I always carried for refueling my lighter. I discovered that the nozzle on the can had opened and leaked its contents over most of my upper leg and groin. This was what had set my skin on fire. I sat for a few moments to try to figure out a way to solve my problem. We had not brought our canteens, so that ruled out washing my leg. The only alternative was to slip my pants down and scrub my leg with fists full of the lush, moist grass we had bedded down on. Buddy was on guard during this time and he crawled over to see what kind of strange ritual I was performing. He almost laughed out loud when I whispered my predicament in his ear.

As I sat in the dark nursing my burning flesh, a sudden "whump" brought my heartbeat to a maddening race. Buddy and I froze as the distant whine of a mortar shell came closer to our position. It whistled over our heads and shattered the dead silence of the night with an earsplitting explosion. Before the echoes of the exploding shell melted away, another round was on its way, this one crashing much closer than the first. Larry jumped straight up from his sleep and tripped over me as I writhed in the grass, struggling to pull up my pants. We huddled behind the fallen walls of the hootch as two more rounds fell into a nearby tree line. We had evidently been detected as we moved into position, because the enemy was definitely firing at us, not at the company perimeter.

Suddenly another mortar tube to our rear coughed loudly, and we knew our platoon was cranking up the little 61mm mortar we had captured in Hai Lang. We were caught directly in the middle as the two mortars fought their private little war. The three of us were scared to death as enemy shells landed all around us and friendly mortar shells arched over our heads to the distant tree line in search of the enemy. We prepared to abandon our listening post as soon as the enemy stopped firing. We gathered our gear, began crawling out of our hiding place, and when the firing stopped, we jumped to our feet and raced through the dark toward friendly positions. Buddy and Larry ran in front, almost blinding me as they pushed past brush and limbs and let them recoil in my face. Drawing closer to the perimeter, we announced our presence with, "Geronimo! Geronimo! Don't shoot! Geronimo!" Suddenly a blinding flash erupted. Larry had snapped the taut wire of a trip flare. Instantly we dove face first to the trail and lay still, hoping our positions would not open up on us, since we had fallen only inches away from the sputtering flare. The white-hot flame soon burned itself out and glowed in the grass like a chunk of red molten metal. We lay still and again called out, "Geronimo!" to the perimeter. A voice called for us to advance, and we picked ourselves up and jogged on through the friendly positions. Once inside the perimeter we learned that Sergeant Sneed had badly burned his hands while rapidly firing the 61mm mortar. He had not taken time to attach the tripod. Instead he had held the tube against the base plate with his bare hands while another GI fed the shells into the weapon.

The next day found us searching the small, deserted villages of Quang Dien. This area depressed us since the villages were all partially destroyed and had grown over with thick vegetation. The VC and NVA were obviously there in numbers. They had turned to psychological tactics of painting anti-American slogans on the walls of some of the hootches and temples. There were racial slogans for the blacks, religious slogans for the Catholics and Jews, and even political slogans about President Johnson. The misspelled words and poorly structured sentences actually gave us a laugh.

In one of the outlying villages we found a strange sight. While searching the torn-down hootches and pagodas of this particular village, someone shouted, "Come here and look at this!" Behind a hootch was a dead water buffalo, which had probably been killed by an artillery shell. He had fallen in his tracks with his head between his knees and the large, curled horns resting on the ground. Maggots had eaten his entire body, leaving his hide draped over the skeleton like a suit of clothes. The ghostly creature stared back at us through empty eye sockets—it was one of those eerie sights one never forgets.

That night we set up a company perimeter among a maze of fighting trenches that the North Vietnamese had obviously dug. We set up our positions just behind one of the zigzagged trenches so we could use it as a foxhole in case of an attack. That was one of our lucky nights, for it turned out that the trenches saved many of us from being listed on the next morning's casualty list. Our squad had chosen a trench that ran parallel to another one ten or twelve feet away. We chose the rear one to set up our positions and started pulling guard, knowing we would probably get hit sometime during the night. We were right. Around two or three o'clock in the morning, our positions were hit by a barrage of hand grenades. The first three exploded simultaneously in the nearby bushes as the enemy probed our perimeter, coaxing us to give away our positions. We knew better than to fire our rifles because of the telltale muzzle flashes, so we started hurling grenades back at the trees to our front. The VC obviously didn't know about our double line of trenches, for they threw another half-dozen grenades into the first trench. We continued to exchange hand grenades. It was nerve-shattering to hear them hit the ground in front of us and slither across the leaves and grass in search of human flesh to lacerate. The enemy had not yet discovered our range and continued to throw most of their weapons short. We crouched in the second line of fighting trenches, praying that the enemy grenades would continue to fall short of their targets. We continued to throw back and forth at each other until one pitifully frightened "cherry" opened up on the tree line with an M60. Then all hell broke loose. It was one of those firefights that you would just as soon sit back and watch, because the fireworks were so beautiful. Tracers from the opposing forces laced a scarlet spider web over the flat terrain, while the yellow and white explosions from RPGs and M79s lit the darkness like giant fireflies. It seemed as though the entire U.S. and NVA armies had met in the dark to do battle as dozens of men fired point-blank into each other's opposing tree lines. The battle continued for more than an hour as the night crawled by. "Papa One," our forward observer for artillery, called in 105mm artillery support since our ammunition was running short. The whining shells slammed hard into the enemy tree line, which lit up with the murderous explosions. The shells were landing so close to us that the shrapnel was zinging over our heads, cutting down the brush and tree limbs that covered our fighting positions. We huddled in the dark, damp trench and let the arty do its job. After an hour or more of bombardment, all was quiet and we waited on the first light of morning.

At daybreak we carefully moved into the enemy lines, which were now a field of stumps and mangled trees. Picking our way through the debris, we counted more than fifteen mutilated bodies that barely resembled human beings. Our company had suffered only one casualty, a minor flesh wound from grenade shrapnel. We had escaped this fight unscathed, and we owed it all to the network of trenches built by our enemy.

After calling in a body count, we moved on toward another village and immediately drew sniper fire. The CO split us up: 1st and 2nd platoons would go straight into the village, and 3rd Platoon around the left flank to enter from the opposite side. We carefully made our way through the thick growth, but stopped when we heard the distant sound of our other two platoons engaging the enemy. It was at least a half-mile away, and Captain Clive radioed for us to move in from the left rear. We started our advance and could hear stray bullets buzzing over the treetops. Our squad was walking point and came to a large canal that lay in a washed-out depression. We were setting up security to cross the canal when a North Vietnamese soldier walked down to the water and began to fill his canteen. We lay in the brush and covered him with our rifles in case he spotted us. Our orders were to move as close as possible without detection, so we quietly watched the soldier from only fifty feet away. After filling his canteen, he stood and looked in our direction; we thought he had detected us, but then he turned toward the distant firing and quickly walked away. We had all thought about shooting him, but couldn't in case his comrades were nearby.

We moved on toward the firefight and were instantly caught up in the battle when an RPG rocket buzzed by Sergeant Sneed, almost hitting him in the head. Everyone dove for cover as another rocket splintered a nearby tree. Handy Matthews and I had thrown ourselves behind a large cluster of bamboo and were trying to get a fix on the source of the rockets' firing. Handy had risen to his knees when another rocket exploded just above our heads, tearing off several stalks of bamboo. He fell across my back and yelled in fear as a white substance covered his black, sweaty face. I gawked in horror, thinking this must be some new kind of chemical warfare weapon and that the two of us would soon be overcome by a toxic acid or debilitating fumes. Handy was scrambling to get away from his rucksack, which seemed to be the origin of the strange chemical, when he realized what the "toxic chemical" was and cursed loudly. His panic had been caused by a punctured can of shaving cream. Handy had put a new can in his pack only a couple of days before; it had been cut in half by a large piece of shrapnel from the enemy rocket, and the cream had spewed out, covering him with mounds of snow-white, lemon-scented lather.

The battle continued for several more minutes until one of our machine-gunners knocked out the enemy position that had been firing the rockets. We cautiously advanced, working our way toward the battle in which the rest of the company was engaged. We had obviously run into an element of battalion size, for they were throwing everything in the

North Vietnamese arsenal at us. A small-caliber antiaircraft gun was turned on us along with .51-caliber machine guns. We had bitten off more than we could chew and quickly withdrew to call for reinforcements. Delta Company was being choppered in while Bravo Company was approaching on foot from two or three miles away. It took a couple of hours to get the other two companies into position, but we knew our enemy was still entrenched within the village because of the sporadic mortar firing that kept harassing us.

Our company was used as a cordoning element to block the southern end of the village while Bravo and Delta pushed in and tried to drive the enemy in our direction. A vicious battle resulted, with our sister companies suffering heavy casualties. Air strikes and artillery pounded the village, and we watched in disbelief as an F4 Phantom screamed in and mistakenly fired its 20mm cannons into the tree line where Bravo Company was holding up. Three dust-off choppers flew sortie after sortie, picking up dead and wounded Americans as the battle raged into the afternoon. The air was filled with smoke and dust and the hum of bullets and shrapnel flying in all directions. Alpha Company held its ground as the persistent enemy soldiers attacked our positions in an all-out effort to escape. We picked them off easily, but also suffered light casualties from their constant firing of mortars and RPG rockets. As we stood our ground, the air suddenly turned foul and began to burn our eyes and throats. "Gas!" was shouted along the defensive positions, and we scrambled to clear our masks and strap them to our heads. We had not received the word that CS grenades were being dropped on the enemy positions from choppers, and were taken by surprise as the potent tear gas drifted over us.

More artillery and air strikes were called in on the North Vietnamese. They were proving to be a tough unit as they held their ground and fought on under the worst conditions possible. The dark of night found us in the same blocking positions. We crawled from our holes and set up trip flares and claymores in an all-out effort to halt the enemy as he tried to escape under darkness. An antique AC47 was called on station to supply us with illumination. It circled continuously overhead, while its crew kicked out three parachute flares with each pass they made. The flares were huge, each one supplying more than a million candlepower of light. As they were tossed out of the lumbering airplane, an automatic trigger mechanism blew off one end while at the same time deploying the parachute and igniting the flare. It was mesmerizing to listen to the drone of the old prop engines and watch the dark sky erupt with the bright-yellow light. The flares were welcomed by us, because they provided the ability to see the enemy as he made his move to escape. The only problem was the likelihood of being hit by the falling trigger mechanism and metal cover that were blown off when each flare ignited. The trigger and cover were attached by a small chain, and they clanged together like a cowbell as they fell toward us from nearly 1,000 feet. The clanging would grow closer and louder, and end abruptly when a loud "whop" announced that the deadly missile had struck the earth and buried itself. All we could do was hope the falling pieces of scrap metal would not hit us.

Scotty, Ken, and I shared the same foxhole; the three of us stayed awake all night staring out across the large rice paddy, hoping to detect the enemy in the eerie light. It was graveyard quiet when suddenly the clanging of a flare detonator grew louder as it sped toward us in the dark. The detonator impacted only a few feet away from our position, and we sighed in relief knowing that the chances of one coming so close again were slim to none. When Ken went out the next morning to gather in our two claymores, he found the flare cover only twelve feet from our foxhole; it had neatly severed the detonator wire to one of the mines.

Joey Miller's squad had moved across the large rice paddy before the flare ship was brought in, and had set up an ambush near the distant tree line. They had settled in along a small canal and lay in the tall grass, hoping to catch small elements of the enemy as they attempted to escape. We knew their location, but a failure in communication had allowed Delta Company's FO to call in artillery near their ambush sight. We lay in the dark and watched in horror as the deadly shells slammed into the tree line, and we could hear our FO desperately trying to contact the battery of howitzers and terminate their fire mission. Another barrage of shells landed exactly where we knew Joey's squad was. The shelling finally stopped, and we waited and wondered about the fate of our fellow soldiers.

Lieutenant Hernandez came crawling over to our foxhole and confirmed that Joey's squad had been hit and had radioed for assistance. The three of us each grabbed a bandolier of ammo and strapped it around our waist as we waited for a radio and a strobe light. A dust-off had already been called, and our mission was to take a medic to the wounded men and help them onto the chopper. A strobe light was needed in order to give the medevac pilot a homing beacon. As soon as we had loaded the wounded, we would lead the rest of the ambush patrol back to safety. I checked the radio, strapped it on my back, and then made one final check with Lieutenant Hernandez to make sure the entire perimeter knew we would be moving across the wide paddy. My major concern was that some of our trigger-happy comrades would see us moving under the light of the flares and fire on us as we traveled the quarter mile across the open ground.

When word was passed down that all had been informed, we started toward the ambush sight. We had gone about 200 yards when a nervous cherry opened up on us from our rear. The tracers from his M16 snapped by us and ricocheted into the night sky. Throwing ourselves into the slimy mud, we screamed out foul profanities toward the company perimeter. A call from our CO immediately came in on the radio saying the problem had been corrected and we would not be receiving any more friendly fire. I acknowledged his transmission and moved our small element on toward tree line. We were nervous as cats as we approached the ambush site. A faint whistle guided us to the crippled squad. What we found was a horrible sight. Two of the GIs had already lapsed into unconsciousness from loss of blood; several others were moaning in the dark with wicked lacerations from shrapnel. One cherry had a hole in his back that I could have put my fist into. A piece of his rib was protruding from it like a long finger. Joey Miller was one of three who had not been hit, but his fear and anger were about to send him into shock. Scotty held a red-lens flashlight as Doc Smith tended to the wounded and asked, "Where the hell is that dust-off chopper?"

I had already switched my radio to the dust-off frequency and soon picked up the deep, guttural voice of the pilot.

"Alpha Three X-ray! This is Dust-off 7. Come in. Over."

"Dust-off 7. This is Alpha Three X-ray. Go ahead."

"Roger, Three X-ray. Thanks for the come back. I'll be in your area in about zero-five. Do you have runway lights? Over."

"Roger. I'll turn 'em on upon your request. Over."

"Roger. Is your Lima Zulu [landing zone] friendly? Over."

"Negative. Over."

"Are you under fire?"

"Negative. Everything's quiet at this moment. Over."

"Are you ready to load your casualties? Over."

"Affirmative. They'll be ready. Over."

"Can you hear my engines? Over."

"Affirmative. Make a left turn at about twenty degrees. Over."

"Roger that. Are you ready with runway lights? Over."

"Roger."

"Okay, Three X-ray! Turn 'em on. I'm coming in."

"Roger! Lights on! Over."

I stood in the rice paddy and clicked on the switch to the small, pocket-size strobe light. I felt naked and lonely as I stood in the dark, holding up a flashing white light that was an easy target for every AK47 in the area. Pressing the radio receiver to my ear, I closed my eyes, thinking it might be better if I couldn't see the tracers racing toward me. No tracers came, and my attention was snapped back into place by the pilot's voice vibrating through the earphone.

"Three X-ray. This is Dust-off 7. I have you in sight. Over."

"Roger, Seven. Come on in. I've got you plenty of room and plenty of passengers. Over."

In less than a minute the loud whopping of the whirling rotor blades descended over the rice paddy and the invisible chopper suddenly lit up as the pilot switched on his landing lights. I stood there holding the strobe light until he landed. I then raced over to the wounded to help lift them onto the hard metal floor of the aircraft.

When all were loaded, I ran around to the pilot's window and gave him the thumbs-up sign. I saw the silhouette of his raised thumb against the red glow of his panel lights. The engines groaned and the dust-off slowly turned and ascended; the wash from the whirling blades pressed our clothes tightly against our bodies.

"Dust-off 7. This is Alpha Three X-ray. Over."

"Go ahead, Three X-ray."

"This is Three X-ray. Thanks for the help. Over."

"Roger that. My pleasure. Just keep your ass down so you won't need us again tonight. Over."

"You can count on that, Seven. Thanks again. Out."

As the chopper engines grew fainter in the distance, we stood huddled in the yellow glow of the flares and planned our next move. Our first responsibility was to gather up the rifles and gear of the evacuated soldiers and help the remainder of the squad back to the company perimeter. Joey Miller felt he should keep the squad at the ambush site, but we convinced him to come back with us and spend the rest of the night within the boundaries of the perimeter.

The next morning we ate a quick can of C's and saddled up to make a push into the village. The enemy—those who had not been killed by air strikes, artillery, or our sister companies—was still holding out in small pockets, so we were prepared to meet some resistance.

We were advancing slowly when a burst of automatic rifle fire raked us from our left flank. One GI fell hard and lay still in the mud as a medic crawled forward to help him. He had been shot through the eagle patch on his left sleeve—the bullet passed through his shoulder and tore out a hole near his spine. He was conscious but in bad shape. The medic hollered for a dust-off. Another freak casualty resulted when a bullet ripped through Roger Thompson's helmet. It entered at an angle and spun around the interior of his helmet liner, digging a deep furrow in his scalp from one ear to the other. Roger was bleeding like a stuck pig, but his wound was not serious and he helped wrap the bandages around his unzipped scalp.

The lone enemy gunner was located and killed, and we continued to move on until we were halted by a wide, deep canal. We were instructed to hold up at the water's edge and wait for Delta Company to push toward us from the opposite direction. As we set up our positions, an M79 grenade launcher was fired a short distance from Ric, Buddy, and me. I turned to see who had fired the shot and caught sight of the gold warhead from a grenade shell as it rolled up the path and stopped at my feet. I froze in my tracks, expecting the projectile to explode at any second while Ric and Buddy dove for cover in the thick brush. Roger Clapeckni had accidentally discharged his M79, and the projectile bounced in front of him, rolling up to our position. We were lucky—the grenade had not traveled far enough to arm itself. It lay at my feet, shining in the sun like a golden egg. Roger came running up to apologize, and we cursed him unmercifully for being so careless. After staring at the grenade for a few seconds, he picked it up, tossed it in the canal, and walked away without saying a word.

The rest of the day was spent cleaning up the few remaining North Vietnamese who had hung on to their defensive positions. Most of them surrendered without a fight. They had suffered greatly under the might of the American war machine, and were willing to give up so as not to go through another day of pounding from artillery and air strikes.

Alpha Company was lucky: this was one battle where our casualties were light. Our sister companies suffered greatly, however. Bravo Company had been chopped up so badly that they were immediately withdrawn from the field and flown back to LZ Sally.

CHAPTER FIVE

AFTER TET

God be with you til we meet again.
By His counsels guide, uphold you
With His sheep, securely fold you.
God be with you til we meet again.

God be with you til we meet again.
Keep love's banner floating o'er you.
Smite death's threatening wave before you.
God be with you til we meet again.

The shaky voices of young American soldiers rose in off-key harmony as they emotionally sang this old hymn. Chaplain Jerry Auten had flown out to the boonies to be with us for a couple of days and hold worship services beneath the shade of the palms and banana trees. He was well liked by all of us, not because we felt being friendly with the chaplain would give us an edge, but because he was the type of fellow who knew everyone's first name and always seemed to cheer us up. His Protestant services were down to earth and were open to everyone—Catholic and Jewish alike.

In his sermons, he seemed to be talking with us rather than preaching. His reading of the scriptures was like poetry and was a soothing relief from the daily crude jargon of combat soldiers. He would close his sermons by having us all stand and sing, "God be with you til we meet again." We would struggle through the verses, without musical accompaniment, all the while knowing that some of us would not be around for the next gathering and singing. To this day, I can't listen to this popular old hymn without getting a lump in my throat.

Captain Auten was different from the other chaplains who would occasionally come to the fields. He carried a CAR-15 assault rifle. One day I asked him why he carried a rifle since it was not SOP for a chaplain. He answered by telling me that he had once watched helplessly as a North Vietnamese, who had not seen him, slaughtered two wounded soldiers. If he had just had a rifle he could have easily killed the enemy soldier, saving the two GI's lives. Since that day, he had deemed it necessary to arm himself when going to the fields.

The Tet Offensive had slowly wound down, and we were now back to engaging small units of VC and company-size elements of North Vietnamese. Because the fighting had decreased somewhat, we could count on one or two firefights a week instead of the devastating five or six a week we had suffered during Tet.

Most of our sunrises were spent listening to "Radio Vietnam," while we heated up a canteen cup of coffee and gagged down a can of ham and limas or ham and eggs for breakfast. "Radio Vietnam" played almost around the clock and came on the air early with a ridiculous program called "Chicken Man." Following that was a two-hour program of the most current popular music—the Beatles, Rolling Stones, Dionne Warwick, Smokey Robinson, and many others. The program was taped in California and the disc jockey was an unknown girl with one of the most tantalizing voices we had ever heard. Her voice ranged somewhere between a whisper and a purr. Listening to her over the airwaves made us terribly homesick for our girlfriends and wives back home. We all tried to imagine what she looked like, finally concluding that she must have buck teeth and weigh about 250 pounds. We still enjoyed her program, and when we had the opportunity we would gather around a beat-up transistor radio, which was taped together and ran off separated cells from an old PRC-25 radio battery.

We continued our "search missions" in Quang Dien and continually engaged elements of Viet Cong and North Vietnamese. One morning as we searched a sparsely populated village, Joe Beckley came sailing over a thick row of hedge as though he had been launched. Behind him came a large, slobbering, red-eyed water buffalo, which charged around the end of the hedgerow and headed straight for us. We scattered like chickens on an interstate highway as the raging beast charged through us, swinging his head from side to side, trying to impale us on his long, curved horns. "Fast Herm" Hope dropped him in his tracks with a quick burst from his M16. The huge animal lay dead in the trail as though glad the chase was over.

Quickly a crowd of villagers gathered, with sharp knives and baskets of woven bamboo. They carved up the buffalo in less than fifteen minutes, leaving nothing but a blood stain where the beast had lain. Meat was a rare source of protein in Vietnam, and whenever an animal was killed in the ongoing conflict, the natives did not let it go to waste.

A few days later we had worked our way to the eastern boundary of the province and were clearing small villages that had been deserted by the civilians. We knew this was extremely dangerous territory because we had heard a report that a paratrooper unit from the 82nd Airborne Division's 3rd Brigade had engaged in a savage firefight in this same group of villages, and had suffered heavy casualties. We moved through the small village where the battle had taken place and found signs of the death and suffering both sides had experienced. I found a helmet with the "fighting-panther" emblem, the symbol of the battalion from the 82nd Airborne Division, drawn on the camouflage cover with a ballpoint pen. There was a bullet hole through both sides of the helmet and a picture of an attractive young girl taped inside. The bottom half of her face bore a pretty smile while the top half of her face was unrecognizable because of the gore that covered it. In disgust, I threw the helmet into a cluster of thick brush. Shredded army fatigues, spent rifle cartridges, bandage wrappers, morphine syringes, and bloody jungle boots were everywhere.

That night we set up just outside the empty village, and Joey Miller was sent in on an ambush patrol with his new squad. The squad had been rebuilt with new replacements from base camp and four or five seasoned men from other squads who had volunteered to join him after his squad was shelled by friendly artillery. They moved out after dark, making their way toward the village square, where they were to hide among the rubble and wait for any enemy troops that might move through the area.

The squad had been away from our perimeter for about thirty minutes when all hell broke loose. Automatic-rifle fire interrupted the still of the night and orange tracers rose skyward from the center of the village. We knew the ambush patrol must be in trouble, but instead of a lingering firefight, suddenly there was silence—the firing stopped just as abruptly as it had started.

Lieutenant Hernandez was frantically trying to reach the squad by radio when Joey called in to inform us of the situation. The "mad minute" of firing occurred when his squad was setting up their ambush at the village square. They were quietly moving around, establishing their positions and fields of fire. A squad of North Vietnamese walked up thinking they had come upon another element of North Vietnamese soldiers. Joey and his men were just as confused as the enemy, for they were suddenly milling about with a lot more bodies than they had started out with. The incident turned comical when the enemy soldiers, still not realizing what was going on, started chatting with the GIs. Frightened beyond words, Joey tried to talk back to the North Vietnamese. That turned the affair into a free-for-all. Everyone suddenly stopped and stared at each other in the dark. Then the enemy soldiers started jabbering and stepping back in the direction from which they had come. The GIs dived for cover and someone opened up on the retreating enemy soldiers with a full burst from his rifle. Wild firing erupted as the squad members fired everything they could at the fleeing enemy. It was said that the enemy soldiers never fired a round, but no one would swear to it since tracers were flying in all directions. Two North Vietnamese died instantly, and another was found the next morning less than fifty yards away.

Joey's squad was lucky: they had survived this bizarre confrontation and were in one piece to talk and laugh about it. But it was no laughing matter at the time. After the firing stopped, they had crawled away from the village square and lay awake all night in thick brush, fearing that more of the enemy would return.

We stayed in the area for a couple more days and then were lifted by Hueys to a new area of operation some twenty miles away. It was similar to the AO we had just left—small, deserted villages controlled by the VC and NVA. Army intelligence informed us that there were two, possibly three, companies of North Vietnamese in the area. A squad of ARVNs (Army of the Republic of Vietnam) was being flown in to work with us, so we held up and took a short break to wait on their chopper. We sure could use them since they supposedly knew the area. When the Huey touched down in a dry field of rice stubble, they poured from the chopper like clowns piling from a compact car at the circus. They looked like boys instead of combat soldiers, but we knew they were well-trained, effective troops. They wore camo fatigues and a hodgepodge of gear. One smiling soldier came over waving his M1 carbine in a friendly fashion. Two chickens, tied together and hanging around his neck, squawked and flapped their wings in a wild frenzy.

We moved to an old fire base that had long since been abandoned. After searching for booby traps, we spent our first night in that unfamiliar territory. As we set up our positions and opened a can of C's, the ARVNs gathered in one corner and built a large fire to cook the chickens, which they had just decapitated. Our CO came over and proceeded to chew them out, making them extinguish their fire and spread out along the perimeter. They chattered in disgust, for now they would not be able to roast their chickens, but they soon gave in and did as ordered.

Lieutenant Hernandez walked over to inform me that I would be taking an ambush to a nearby village. My squad was reluctant because of the unfamiliar terrain, but I assured them we would try to avoid the villages while moving toward our destination. We waited until total darkness before leaving the safety of the company perimeter. Then we quietly slipped into the black night. Movement was slow—we spent more than an hour following an old roadbed that bisected the vast fields of rice paddies. The road was paralleled by two drainage ditches, and we felt safe using them as our avenue of approach to the villages. We moved down these trenches, keeping a low profile, and stopped to send out a reconnaissance patrol as we approached the first hamlet. Ric and Buddy Travino crept to the edge of the village and came back with a report that they could hear voices coming from inside the tree line. We knew there were no civilians in the area, so the voices must be those of the enemy. I wasn't about to take my squad at night into an unfamiliar area that was known to be inhabited by the enemy, so we pulled back to a small canal and discussed our next move.

I called Lieutenant Hernandez and informed him we would be moving beyond this village to a different ambush site. I had chosen a distant road crossing as an alternate site. I had studied the map thoroughly before leaving the company perimeter, so without using a flashlight to read my map, I guessed at the approximate grid coordinates for our new destination. This was a mistake that almost cost us our lives.

I gave the lieutenant the grid of our new location, and we moved there. After making a quick check of our ambush site, we quietly settled in for a long night. Bud and Roger took rear security while the rest of us trained our weapons on the nearby trails. We had to lie in the open, since the only cover nearby was a low-profile dike. As it turned out, this small dike would save our lives, as the horrifying events of the night began to unfold.

Unbeknownst to us, the CO had received orders to move the company to the edge of one of the nearby villages. This move was to take place during the middle of the night so they could maneuver on a suspected company of North Vietnamese during the early-morning hours of the next day. Our ambush site lay directly in the path of our entire company as they moved out for their early-morning assault. I had mistakenly given the lieutenant the wrong grid and the CO figured us to be at another crossroad a quarter-mile away. Therefore he did not feel it necessary to inform us of their move.

The night was half spent and our squad lay quietly behind the dike, staring off into the darkness. A third of us slept while the others stood guard against any enemy movement on the trails to our front. I was awakened by a shake of my shoulder and a hand clasped over my mouth. Roger Clapeckni crouched beside me, and I instantly sensed danger as he motioned toward the road crossing. I peered over the dike and was horrified to see shadowy figures less than thirty yards away— dozens of soldiers were moving past us at a quick pace. Bud Dykes whispered in my ear that he estimated there were around a hundred of them.

I dared not use the radio to call for help, and quickly reached for the control knobs on the PRC-25 to turn off the squelch so the noise wouldn't give away our position. We lay frozen in the darkness and watched as the silent figures moved past us and disappeared in the ebony shadows. If they had been thirty yards closer they would have walked directly over us, forcing us to initiate a deadly firefight. Since we were greatly outnumbered, we chose to let them pass—attempting an ambush would have meant suicide for us. The troops continued to move past our position, and we listened to their footsteps, completely unaware that they were our friends and comrades from Alpha Company. Our plan was to let the enemy pass, then slip quietly back toward the company compound before making radio contact.

After the last of the column of soldiers had drifted away in the dark, we lay motionless for several minutes. Then we quickly gathered our grenades and gear and slithered like reptiles to the drainage ditches that lay between us and our ambush "kill zone." We crawled for at least fifty yards in the dry canals before climbing out and running like hell along the road. We stopped for a minute to make radio contact, but I was unable to raise anyone on the PRC-25, since the entire company was maintaining radio silence as they moved through the darkness. We decided to return to the company perimeter to inform the CO of the enemy troop movement.

Trying another transmission on the radio with negative contact, we moved to within shouting distance of the fire base and broke the silence with, "Geronimo! Geronimo! Don't shoot! Geronimo!"

A friendly voice called out for us to advance, and we jogged forward to rendezvous with one of our soldiers at the entrance to the barbed-wire perimeter. As we entered the perimeter, he told us of the company's departure and informed us that we were now the only ones in the deserted fire base, besides his squad, left to guard the extra equipment. The puzzle pieces—massive troop movement and no radio contact— were now falling together, and I nearly grew sick with the horrifying thought of how close we had come to ambushing our own company. My mistake had nearly caused a tragedy. I was lucky—it could have been a fatal error. I had learned my lesson the hard way: never second-guess a map, especially in the dark.

We dispersed around the perimeter and spent the next few hours wondering about the fate of our friends. They were moving toward one of the most vicious firefights in which Alpha Company would ever participate.

Before dawn, large shells from distant guns began falling in the small villages to our front. The assault had started. For the next half hour the 105mm and 155mm shells screamed over our heads and slammed into the tree lines, which now grew visible in dawn's first light. Somewhere out there Alpha Company stalked her prey like a lioness and would spring into action the instant the last artillery shell sounded. The smell of exploding powder and burning hootches drifted over us as we watched from our secure positions. I made a call to the CO and asked if he wanted us to join them, but his reply was negative since they would have to hold up their forward progress to wait on us. He instructed me to hold my squad in reserve in case we were needed later on, so we settled back with nothing to do but watch and pray for our fellow soldiers.

The shelling stopped; for a few minutes there was silence as we stared out over the rice paddies through the smoke and early-morning mist. A single rifle began to cough out short bursts of automatic fire;

then dozens more joined in and several machine guns rattled in the background. Muffled explosions from M79s could be heard against the commanding explosions of mortar shells as the firefight grew louder and louder. I turned up the volume on our radio so we could keep track of the battle, and we sat silently, listening to the three platoon leaders call each other as they maneuvered through the village.

A call for a dust-off told us that Alpha Company had already suffered casualties, and then another lieutenant called in asking for two medevac choppers instead of one. We felt helpless as we listened to the battle unfolding less than a half-mile away. The fighting raged on as two dust-off choppers flew in, disappearing below the tree line. They soon lifted from the village and flew directly over us on their way to the 22nd Surg at Phu Bai. We could see medics crouching over the mounds of wounded and dead soldiers who had been quickly piled into the choppers.

Bud shouted that two enemy soldiers were running across a distant rice dike, coming our way. We strained our eyes to pick them out of the smoke and waited for them to come closer. Every member of our small party trained his weapon on the two advancing soldiers and then opened up in unison as they came within effective range. They were both hit instantly by hundreds of M16 rounds, which seemed to hold them in suspension for a few seconds and then violently throw them backwards into the rice paddy.

The firefight raged on for hours as air strikes, artillery, and Cobra gunships decimated the village. Several more dust-off choppers visited Alpha Company that day and decreased its numbers by extracting the dead and wounded. Sergeant Leroy Mullins led his squad into the midst of a group of burning hootches and was attacked by several NVA hurling Chi-Com grenades. The entire squad was wounded, and Sergeant Mullins lost several toes when a razor-sharp chunk of steel tore off the end of his jungle boot. The medevacs continued to roar in and lift out casualties as the battle continued. One chopper with a large red cross on its side had just touched down to receive a load of wounded GIs when an 80mm mortar shell landed beneath its whirling rotor blades and blew off half of one of the blades. The dust-off vibrated violently as the pilots tried to get airborne. They shut down their engines when they realized their predicament. The enemy gunners continued to pour shells on the crippled bird in an effort to finish it off. Two of the wounded were killed instantly as a shell screamed into the banana trees where they had been carried by the medics.

The day dragged on; the savage battle continued to make statistics out of both friend and foe. The enemy mortar teams were the greatest menace to our troops as they fired shell after shell into our lines. Lieutenant Hernandez and his RTO were burned slightly when they threw themselves into a small crater that had been dug by a white phosphorous shell. The shell had impregnated the loosened earth with smoldering phosphorus, which stuck to their skin and clothes as they wallowed in the dirt.

Finally a call came for us to advance and join the company—the day was almost over and they needed our help. It took most of an hour to reach them. We rendezvoused in time to help load several wounded GIs onto the last dust-off of the day.

It was decided that we would set up a company perimeter around the downed chopper to prevent the enemy from moving in and destroying it during the night. Plans had been made for a flying crane to come in the next day and lift out the medevac chopper; our job was to protect it until the extraction was completed.

As dusk fell we worked diligently to dig holes and set out flares and claymores as a defensive measure against a possible night attack. A fellow North Carolinian, Tray Efird, was humped over an E-tool (small army shovel), feverishly digging the foxhole in which he would spend the night, when a dazed and wounded North Vietnamese walked right up to his position in the semidarkness with an AK in his hand. Tray thought the soldier standing over him was a fellow GI until the dazed North Vietnamese spoke. Tray froze in his tracks and glared into the fading light. The enemy soldier spoke again, and by this time Tray was going for his forty-five. Tray was a machine-gunner, and also carried a .45-caliber pistol in a side holster in case he needed a smaller weapon for close combat. His M60 was sitting just a couple of feet away, but would have been too bulky to try to use before the NVA realized what was happening. He snatched the pistol from the holster, cocked the hammer, and fired point-blank into the chest of the young soldier, killing him instantly. This incident had served as a warning: we would have to pull 100 percent alert because a large number of enemy troops still remained in the village.

Most of us were well dug in when total darkness blanketed the village. Three LPs were sent out for advance warning, and Bud was chosen to take one out in front of our perimeter sector. He picked Ric and Roger, and the three of them slid silently into the dark surroundings to make their way toward the far side of a large vegetable garden. I coordinated directions with Bud, since they would be positioned directly in front of our squad and might have to charge back toward us if things became too hot.

Several hours had elapsed when two nearby explosions woke me from a light sleep. Hud Bowers and I were sharing a foxhole. He quickly grabbed me by the collar as I slept beside our fighting position and dragged me face first into the foxhole. As we grabbed for our rifles, Bud and his LP team came charging over us yelling, "Geronimo! Don't shoot!" Ric was running so hard that he fell directly into our foxhole and nearly knocked out Hud with the butt of his rifle.

Between gasps for breath, Bud told us what happened: they had set up their LP at the base of a large tree, and an enemy soldier had climbed out of the tree and dropped directly in the middle of them as they lay in the scrub brush. I couldn't help laughing as I visualized the incident and how scared that poor North Vietnamese must have been when he realized what he had done. Bud said the soldier ran around in circles, stepping all over them before he scrambled off into the bushes. The two explosions came from grenades they had managed to throw at the enemy soldier as he crashed through the undergrowth in his attempt to escape.

The rest of the night was quiet. As dawn approached we welcomed the new day with hopes that the enemy had escaped during the night so that we could get some rest and not have to confront him in the still-smoldering village. Later in the morning, the downed chopper was lifted out, and we stayed in the area to wait on a Huey bringing us a new Vietnamese Kit Carson scout. When the slick touched down, a small figure jumped off, and we all laughed at what appeared to be a young boy in army fatigues about ten sizes too large for him. As he approached we could see he was a kindly faced young man who stood only five feet tall. His name was Van Long, and he had come over to fight against the communists after serving them as a VC for three years. He was soft spoken and knew very little English. This made it extremely difficult to benefit from his efforts. He simply tagged along for the first few days. Bud and I quickly became his best friends as we made an effort to help him with his English, and he in turn taught us a few phrases in Vietnamese. We ordered him the smallest pair of fatigues our supply sergeant could find, and also helped him rearrange his gear so it wouldn't fall off every time he ran for cover. Van Long was intelligent and quick to learn. He soon became an asset to our company as we struggled from day to day through the perils of combat.

We continued our search-and-clear missions in the small, deserted villages and could always count on making some degree of enemy contact, from a single VC sniper to company-size elements of North Vietnamese. One day we humped the rice paddies until noon in an effort to reach a small hamlet we had not searched before. After a quick break for a can of C's, each platoon went in different directions to surround the quiet, lonely little village. The Third Herd moved around to the rear of the target area and began a slow sweep through the clusters of blown-down hootches and the overgrown paths leading toward the village square. We found countless signs of enemy activity and began torching the intact hootches, which were obviously being used by the NVA.

The sensation of danger hung in the air. Our fears were confirmed when the 1st Platoon made enemy contact on the far side of the village. We spread out even more and, avoiding clearings, we continued our movement toward the ensuing firefight. A nearby burst of automatic-rifle fire put us all on our bellies while the chatter of rifles increased to a steady roar. Our squad had managed to take cover behind a small stone wall surrounding a pagoda, and I held them there waiting on instructions from Lieutenant Hernandez. A quick shout to Joey Miller's squad gave me the news that no one could locate the lieutenant. Then the shattering report was passed along to us that he had possibly been hit. I told my squad to stay put while I moved forward to try to locate our platoon leader and his RTO.

I had gone about thirty yards in the general direction of the rifle fire when more firing forced me to take cover. I could hear the shouting of GIs and realized that the 2nd Platoon was not far away. Moving on at a very cautious pace, I caught a glimpse of a North Vietnamese struggling to climb from his spider hole. He was bleeding profusely from the neck and chest. In his efforts, he did not notice me hiding in the thick undergrowth. Concerned that some of his comrades might be in the immediate area, I chose to lob a grenade at him instead of giving away my position by firing my M16. My heart was about to jump up into my throat as I fumbled with the safety pin and finally cleared it from the firing mechanism. The enemy soldier was still struggling to climb from his fighting position when I pitched the grenade toward him and watched it roll up to his knees. I ducked below the brush to avoid the shrapnel, and when I arose seconds later, he had disappeared and smoke and dust were settling on the still-trembling underbrush. I waited for a moment and then raced forward to inspect the small bunker. The concussion had killed the young soldier instantly and forced his body back into the spider hole. He lay crumpled at the bottom. I grabbed his arm and pulled him out so I could search for weapons. There beneath him was a brand-new SKS assault rifle that looked as though it had just come from the shipping case. The cast-aluminum bayonet was fixed in the fighting position. I quickly snapped it back along the barrel and slung the rifle over my back.

A friendly voice shouted from a distance, asking me to check on Lieutenant Hernandez, but I had no idea where he was. Specialist, Fourth Class Bill Thompson, from the 2nd Platoon, came running up and reported that they had seen Lieutenant Hernandez and his RTO walk blindly into an enemy position while others had tried in vain to shout a warning. The 2nd Platoon was aware of this enemy position but had been unable to destroy it. Thompson told me that an NVA soldier had fired point-blank at Lieutenant Hernandez, but they lost sight of him as they fired back at the enemy. Wayne Timmons, the RTO, had escaped and scrambled back toward the waiting platoon.

I raced back to my squad, where I received the devastating news that our lieutenant had been killed and that the 2nd Squad was carrying out his body. I later found out that the rifle I captured was the one that had killed Lieutenant Hernandez. I was torn between throwing the rifle into a river or keeping it out of respect for its victim.

The firefight raged on for another hour. We withdrew to the edge of the village to let the artillery do its job and to extract our dead and wounded. Sergeant Sneed had also been wounded, but he took charge of our platoon and moved us around the village to link up with the rest of the company. I asked where Lieutenant Hernandez's body was, and a soldier from the 1st Platoon pointed toward a hedgerow where three soldiers lay rolled up in ponchos. Bud and I walked over to the bodies and learned that Lieutenant Scott and Private First Class Garcia had also died in the firefight. We wanted to pay our last respects, so we knelt and uncovered the face of our fallen leader. Bud and I were devastated by what we saw: he had been hit six or eight times in the face, and his ghostlike expression reflected the fear he had felt just before his horrible and sudden death. His teeth were all missing, and shards of glass from his shattered eyeglasses protruded from a bullet hole just below his eyebrow. I felt a sudden urge to vomit as I choked back the lump in my throat. While we knelt there in silence, Sfc. "Pat" Patterson from the 2nd Platoon walked over and placed his hands on our shoulders. He knew how deeply we felt about Lieutenant Hernandez. He told us to go back to our squad and assured us his men would take care of things.

We slowly made our way back to the 3rd Platoon, stopping to console the wounded soldiers who lay in the grass waiting on a medevac chopper. I was surprised to learn that our CO had been hit several times in the legs; one of his RTOs had also been hit. It had been a bad day for us, with the death of two officers and a third wounded, plus several privates, specialists, and buck sergeants on our casualty list. The enemy had dealt us a severe blow with minimum losses of his own.

Bud and I were assigned as acting platoon sergeant and platoon leader, because Sergeant Sneed was also extracted due to his shrapnel wounds. Our only other E-6, Bill Rollins, had left the field several days earlier due to medical problems. Our platoon was now in the hands of two buck sergeants. We were the best of friends and were confident we could lead our platoon until a new officer and noncom were assigned to us.

Several days passed as we continued our search-and-clear mission through the small, abandoned villages. Enemy contact was minimal. Our only casualty resulted when Scotty foolishly cut open an RPG rocket charge he had found and lit the powder with a cigarette lighter. He had poured the black powder in a long trail and thought it would burn slowly enough for him to move out of its way. Just as he held the lighter to the powder, an unexpected change in the wind blew the spewing flames toward him, cooking his face and hands. Bud and I expressed our disgust and anger, cursing him for inflicting such an unnecessary injury. Our fighting strength was extremely low, and we needed all the manpower available. One look at Scotty's swollen face assured us that the medics were right when they called for a dust-off.

On one of our daily log ships, which brought our supplies, mail, and ammo, a young, overweight first lieutenant arrived. He asked where he could find the 3rd Platoon. His name was Walt Melton, and he was to be our new platoon leader. He had a casual sort of personality and immediately put us at ease with his nonchalant attitude toward the war. He seemed to know his responsibilities, and he demanded our respect, but he also handled his position as just another job—he did the best he could and said to hell with the rest.

His first night with us found our company setting up a night defensive perimeter in a large graveyard. We had moved into the edge of Phuoc Yen, which would be our area of operation for the next few weeks. The new lieutenant informed me I would be taking a squad ambush into the nearby villages and showed me on my map where we were to go.

When night had fallen, our squad gathered the essential gear needed for our patrol and moved out under the dark, overcast sky. We made our way slowly into the village, since there was no light from the blanketed moon and stars. Reaching our destination, we settled in just in time to hear the distant thundering of enemy mortar shells. Our company had come under attack. A quick radio message confirmed they were under a heavy mortar attack, but the numerous grave mounds that the GIs were huddled behind should prevent casualties.

We pulled 100 percent alert for the first three or four hours, and were scared badly when Buddy Travino fired a burst of tracers at something that raced across his field of fire. He swore it was five or six feet tall and carried a weapon, but a close inspection the next morning turned up a large, mangy dog with a bullet hole through its head.

When we returned to the company, our new CO informed our lieutenants that headquarters was moving us into Phuoc Yen, where the 9th Battalion of the 90th NVA Regiment had been found. The Song Bo River snaked its way through the village and formed a large horseshoe at the southern end. Our enemy had committed a grave mistake and allowed themselves to be trapped within the horseshoe; several paratrooper companies were being rushed in to seal off the area. Along with three paratrooper infantry companies, there was a Black Panther Company from the 1st ARVN Division plus three platoons of local popular forces (PFs). Within six hours, we had all moved into position and begun one of the most devastating operations the North Vietnamese would encounter. It was a classic cordoning operation: we had the enemy trapped and surrounded. We would use one element to move in and force him to try to exfiltrate through the surrounding forces.

We lined the banks of the Song Bo with positions located about fifty feet apart. The first day, April 28th, was spent digging foxholes on the riverbank while artillery and air strikes pulverized Phuoc Yen. I clearly remember that particular day because it was my birthday and my squad took a break from building fighting positions to give me a party. While nearby artillery shrapnel from across the river buzzed over our heads and snipped branches from the trees, several sweaty GIs sang "Happy Birthday" to me, presenting their version of a cake—a rounded chunk of turkey loaf from a C-rat can with Q-tips soaked in mosquito lotion for candles. I received as gifts a pack of Pall Malls; a pack of gum with one stick missing; a new bottle of mosquito lotion; one grenade; and a pair of clean, dry socks. This was, without a doubt, the most memorable birthday party I had ever had.

Our first night was one of taut nerves and squinted eyes—we knew the enemy soldiers would be trying to swim the river in an attempt to escape. A flare ship, soaring above us in the black night, dropped large parachute flares. Several hours had passed with no sight of the enemy when one of our squad members crawled down to my position and informed me that several enemy soldiers were attempting to swim the river. They would soon be coming ashore in front of his position. Bud and I crawled along the riverbank with the other GI and lay quietly in the brush, watching four heads bobbing slowly toward us in the eerie light. We decided to grab them as they crawled out of the water. They would be exhausted from their swim and should put up little resistance. Evidently one of them detected us as we crouched on the riverbank, for he spoke to the others and they quickly turned around, heading back for the far side of the river. Realizing they had seen us, we stood and shouted "Come here!" in Vietnamese. This only frightened them, however. They filled their lungs and dove under the water. We waited for them to bob up, then fired warning shots while shouting orders for their surrender. We had mixed emotions about shooting them, since they were more than likely unarmed. Yet, they were the enemy, and if they continued to swim away from us, there would be only one thing left to do. They stayed close together, continuing to bob up for air one by one, and were getting closer to the far side of the river. If we let them reach the opposite shore, they could easily hide under the thick brush that leaned from the banks and dipped its branches into the gliding river currents.

The decision was made—"Shoot!" We trained our rifles on the glassy, black water and fired full automatic at each struggling head as the enemy soldiers burst through the surface and gasped for air. When the firing ceased and the waters calmed, they had all disappeared into a cold, wet grave. We stood on the bank and mulled over how we would rather have captured them alive instead of slaughtering them, as they had forced us to do.

Bud and I moved back to our position, and I could tell he felt just as badly about the incident as I did. I tried to convince myself that we had done the right thing, but the thought of killing those helpless soldiers would haunt me for years to come.

Early the next day a Huey flew in with an emergency load of ammunition. The chopper settled down in an old garden spot, and there, sitting on stacked cases of ammunition, was someone we had been looking for for a long time—Sfc. Eddie Hands was back. The news of his return spread fast. Before he could run out from under the wash of the rotor blades, several of us had run up to greet him with outstretched hands and slaps on the back. He had gained several pounds and looked rested. He seemed to be as glad to see us as we were to see him. We introduced him to Lieutenant Melton, and then moved back to our positions along the riverbank.

The battle for Phuoc Yen lasted five days. On the final day, the remaining small pockets of enemy soldiers surrendered to the ARVN Black Panthers. We had dealt the enemy a crushing blow. This highly successful operation would greatly lessen the constant threat to the city of Hue. The final enemy body count was near 440, with 145 of the enemy surrendering during the last two days of the battle.

This had been an easy one for Alpha Company—our task had been simply to serve as a blocking force while other companies of GIs and ARVNs did all the dirty work. Our last few hours at Phuoc Yen were spent dividing up a chopperload of cherries, assigning them to the platoons and squads that were drastically understrength. The cherries had brought with them a bright-red sack of mail, bulging with letters and packages. Mailbags usually boosted our morale, but this one brought bad news to Sergeant Larry Young and me. We both received what every soldier has always joked about—Dear John letters. His was from his wife; mine was from the girl who was to marry me when my army hitch was over. Larry and I moped around for awhile, trying to make jokes about the letters, but I knew he must be suffering more than I, since he had lost a wife, not just a girlfriend.

CHAPTER SIX

EIGHT-KLICK VILLE

Following the battle of Phuoc Yen, several days were spent searching and clearing the many small villages in the deltas south of Hue. The weather was becoming as big an enemy as the North Vietnamese and "Charlie Cong," with temperatures exceeding 100 degrees and humidity in the high 90 percent range. We moved south for almost a week with little resistance from the enemy, but the heat was draining our strength. Our new CO, Captain Keever, would work us for two hours, then give us an hour to lie in the shade of the banana trees and let the sweat evaporate from our drenched fatigues. We were told we would soon reach a new AO, a Viet Cong–controlled area near the coast. No American forces had been there before, so army intelligence had little information for us.

This area of operation lay in the vast rice deltas that sprawled between Highway One and the coastal sand dunes; it was a long, narrow strip of villages bordering both sides of a small river. The hamlets were connected to each other and gave the appearance of one long village stretching for more than eight kilometers. Because of its size, our new AO was dubbed "Eight-Klick Ville." The northern end of Eight Klick was heavily populated, but the further south we went the fewer civilians we encountered. We were informed that there were practically no NVA in the area, but that we should expect to find a few Viet Cong who were natives of the nearby villages. We accepted this information with little concern, but the next three months would prove to be the worst of the entire year. We would soon learn to hate Eight-Klick Ville passionately and curse its name with vulgar adjectives. It was an area full of booby traps, snipers, VC patrols, and civilians sympathetic to the enemy. It would drain our morale, inflict heavy casualties, and instill in all of us a hatred for guerrilla warfare. Most of us had maintained a certain degree of sympathy for the natives and tried to help them whenever possible, but the torment, death, suffering, and harassment that "Eight-Klick Ville" dealt out to us soon changed our attitudes to distrust, hatred, and violence.

The first two days in the area were spent in the northern end of the ville as we worked our way among the civilians, who attempted to act as though they weren't nervous about our presence. I remember watching a woman preen the hair of a young girl; I turned my head in disbelief as she ate the tiny lice she plucked from the child's silky black hair. She had no way of knowing how disgusting this appeared to us. It was a common practice among the peasants, the only means they had to rid themselves of the pesky parasites.

Head lice were not the only parasites that seemed to abound in Eight Klick. The river and small canals were full of green and brown leeches that grew up to ten inches long. They were nasty little creatures, much more aggressive than land leeches. Whenever we waded in the water, we invariably became covered with the leeches, which found openings in our clothing and snaked their way inside to sink their ugly faces into our flesh. It was not uncommon to pull ten or twelve from our legs and buttocks and to find just as many on our clothing. They crawled all over us in search of an unbloused pant cuff or tear in our fatigues. One morning while stooping over the warm, dirty water of a flooded rice paddy, I watched several of the ugly creatures swim up to my hands as I prepared to shave. Each time I swished my razor in the water, dozens of leeches would swim around in a wild frenzy, smelling the sweat and shaving cream I had scraped from my face and neck. By the time I had finished shaving, at least thirty of them were cruising around, waiting for anything that fell into the water. In disgust, I pulled a full bottle of mosquito repellent from my shirt pocket and gave them a drink of the alcohol-laden lotion.

As we worked the hamlets in Eight-Klick Ville, Van Long seemed increasingly nervous with each passing day. He conversed with the natives and verbally lashed out at them, obviously disagreeing with their feelings about our presence. He would walk away mumbling, "VC numba ten!" Occasionally he would slap a woman or old man across the face.

On a hot, stifling afternoon, we received word to unchamber the rounds in our weapons—our new battalion commander was flying in to see us. Everyone expressed disbelief at this nonsensical order; we jacked the rounds from their chambers, only to slip another one in as soon as the lieutenants turned their backs. A Huey soon flew in and dropped off our new battalion CO, Colonel Huntley. He was a "bird colonel" who went by the call sign "White Falcon." His deep tan, salt-and-pepper hair, and tall, sinewy physique gave him the appearance of being in command of any situation. When he walked out in the brush to chat with us, his two RTOs seemed scared to death—obviously they had heard about the wall-to-wall booby traps in the area. He asked us about our supplies, food, and mail, and wanted to know if there were any complaints he could take care of. One GI jokingly asked if he could manage to get a peace treaty signed with North Vietnam; another asked him why we had to unchamber a round in our rifles whenever a commanding officer came to the fields. His comment to that question was, "Bullshit!" He immediately informed our company officers that this foolish command was to be abolished. It seemed this rule was established back when our brigade first arrived in the country, and no one had bothered to question it when a change of command took place. We were pleased to know we were responsible for informing the new commander of this dangerous rule, and particularly pleased because he had listened to us and acted on our complaint. He had done what he had set out to do—win the confidence of his troops. From that day forward we welcomed his visits and never questioned orders that came from battalion headquarters.

After a few days of constant searching and clearing, the few civilians in the area became familiar with our operational procedures and patterns of movement. They could figure out approximately where we would be the next day and then have the VC move in the night before and saturate the area with land mines and booby traps. It took us almost a week to figure out why we would receive a mortar attack every night shortly after we set up our perimeter. Someone finally realized that our problem stemmed from a small "buffalo boy" who rode on the back of one of the large animals he tended during the day. He nonchalantly grazed his animals and followed us as we moved through the hamlets, keeping his small herd just outside the tree lines and letting them feed on the grassy edges of the rice fields and graveyards. From under his conical hat he watched every move we made. He would disappear just before dark, obviously to report our position to the local Viet Cong. They stayed clear of us during the day, but when night came would sneak up to where the young boy directed them and fire several mortar shells into our perimeter before slinking away to safety.

Determined to end this harassment, we allowed the buffalo boy to follow us to our NDP (night defensive position). Just as he turned his small herd to disappear into the evening shadows, we sent out four GI's to stop him and bring him to our perimeter. He was scared to death. I felt sorry for him since he was so young and defenseless, but he was aiding the enemy. Regardless of our sympathy, he would have to be dealt with.

Van Long questioned him and soon had him crying in fear. We had no intention of hurting him, but he didn't know this, so we let him talk and inform us of the VC elements in the area. He confessed to spying on us and reporting our position to the Cong. He explained that his family would be in jeopardy if he did not cooperate with the VC. We kept him with us during the night and for the first time in more than a week we received no mortar attack.

The next day, tragedy struck our squad. We were spread over a large area of hootches and garden plots, moving quickly through the bamboo hedgerows, stopping only to look for booby traps. Bud had half of the squad and was working near a canal. I had the other half and was clearing out several thatched hootches. We had stopped to take a quick break for a swig of water and a cigarette when a grenade went off down by the canal. Rifle shots rang out followed by a shout for a medic. When we reached our buddies we found three or four of them standing over Scotty, who was writhing on the ground and clutching his blood-covered stomach. No one had seen exactly what happened, but from what we could gather, Scott had flushed a VC from his hiding place and had taken a gut full of hot shrapnel when the enemy soldier rolled a grenade near his feet. He was in bad shape and could hardly talk but managed to tell us that the Viet Cong had escaped into the thick growth near the banks of the canal. No one had seen the Cong. He would be back again to take another crack at those of us who remained in his territory.

We were becoming so paranoid about booby traps that we were afraid to leave the trails and perform our search-and-clear duties as they needed to be done. One morning we approached an old concrete foot-bridge over a lily-covered canal. We had used this footbridge many times in the past couple of weeks, but today we were halted by a large heap of bamboo brush piled on the bridge. We would not be able to use the bridge without clearing away the brush, but the barrier had us puzzled and nervous because it reeked of danger.

An old and extremely feeble man stood nearby, watching us as we contemplated our next move. Someone suggested that we get him to clear away the brush, since most of the civilians knew where the booby traps were located. Lieutenant Melton sent a couple of our troops to fetch the old man so Van Long could question him. The man reminded me of a delicate porcelain figurine. His brown, weathered skin hung loosely over a skeleton that almost protruded at every joint of his body. He wore dirty white silk pants with a shirt that clung to his frame and hung to his knees. His head was almost bald and his face bore patches of what was once a wiry gray beard and goatee.

He and Van Long jabbered back and forth until finally the old man stepped onto the bridge and reluctantly moved toward the bamboo barrier. He shuffled forward, finally reaching the brush pile. Then slowly he turned and looked at us as if to beg, "Please let me come back!" Van Long ordered him on, and the old fellow reached forward to grab a branch of bamboo. He tugged slightly and nothing happened as he freed the limb and tossed it into the canal. We stood quietly and watched as he grabbed another branch and gave it a quick jerk. As he pulled it from the pile, an orange flash and tremendous explosion pelted us with bamboo slivers and knocked all of us on our backs. The old man disappeared in a white cloud of smoke and dust. When I looked up, he was gone. Someone shouted that he was floating facedown among the lily pads, which were still dancing on the rippling water. A couple of our men tore off their gear and jumped in to retrieve the old man. A small crowd of civilians gathered as two of our medics worked over him, giving him mouth-to-mouth resuscitation. He was badly burned, and bled from several holes in his chest and head, gouged by chunks of the concrete bridge. An old woman rushed up and threw herself down beside him, crying and wailing a Vietnamese death chant. He was still alive but failing fast. A medevac chopper was called in, so we carried him to a clearing to wait on the dust-off. The fragile old woman continued her wailing and moaning. There was not much the medics could do for this old gentleman; he expired just moments before the dust-off lumbered in to pick him up. We loaded the old couple onto the chopper and watched the lady still flailing her arms and hands as the chopper flew out of sight. It had been a sad experience, but one we would have to forget. We turned back toward the bridge and moved on across.

Each passing day brought more casualties to Alpha Company: troopers stepped on land mines, triggered explosive devices concealed in lush vegetation, and impaled their feet and legs on treacherous punji stakes that seemed to be everywhere. Eight Klick was becoming a ghost town —the few civilians who had stayed after our arrival were now leaving because of constant harassment by the VC and the growing number of booby traps that even they did not know about. We continued our monotonous chores of searching and clearing the hamlets, trying to hang on to our composure though it was constantly challenged by the ingenuity and determination of Charlie Cong.

The constant tension was taking its toll on us. Since we got little sleep at night, we grew more and more careless working our way through the VC-infested hamlets. One night, after moving in the dark for more than an hour, we set up our perimeter in a large graveyard overgrown with knee-deep grass. The CO came around and instructed the platoon leaders about our positions. Upon his orders, we began settling down behind the mounds and establishing our fields of fire. The sky was overcast, which made our visibility poor. We lay in the soft, damp grass and glared out into the total darkness. Three or four hours had passed when Barry White woke me and whispered that he had seen movement in front of our position. I rose to my knees and stared into the void surrounding us. Barry swore he had seen a figure walk a short distance in front of us and then crouch down as though trying to hide. Taking no chances, I crawled back to our platoon CP and informed Lieutenant Melton of the possibility of enemy movement in front of our perimeter. I requested that he radio the company CO to have an illumination round fired from our 61mm mortar tube at the command post. Crawling back to my position, I informed Barry and Sgt. Larry Young that we would soon have illumination, enabling us to find out if there really was enemy movement. The three of us were crouched behind our large grave mound, staring out into the blackness, when a definite movement startled us into reality. It appeared to be a human figure crouching in the grass not more than sixty or seventy feet away. Where in the hell is that illumination? raced through my mind as I clutched my rifle and reached for a grenade. Seconds seemed like hours as we waited on the "thump" of our mortar tube, which would send a parachute flare arching over our heads; but it never came.

Again there was movement and I decided to take matters into my own hands. I rose to my knees and shouted, "Who goes there!" The ghostlike figure immediately sprawled flat in the tall grass and did not answer my challenge. This was all I needed. I yanked the safety pin from the grenade and threw my best pitch toward the target, which had now disappeared. A bright yellow flash stabbed the darkness as the grenade exploded and alerted the rest of our perimeter. The three of us fixed our rifles on the target area. In less than five seconds, a burst of orange tracers snapped out of the night, missing our heads by only inches. An explosive projectile slammed into our grave mound and threw dirt and grass all over us. Barry yelled, "Son of a bitch! Now we've made the whole North Vietnamese Army mad at us!" More tracers popped by our heads as yet another explosive projectile buzzed by our grave mound and exploded somewhere near the platoon CP. When there was a slight lull in the firing, the three of us jumped up and sprayed the area with automatic bursts from our M16s. Another retaliation delivered more rifle slugs and explosives into our position, covering us with another layer of moist dirt and clumps of grass. More fire was exchanged until finally a sharp command of, "Cease fire!" echoed over the din of the small battle. Again, "Cease fire!" was shouted as an illumination round blossomed over our heads and drifted from a small silk parachute through the cool night air.

Lieutenant Melton and Sergeant Hands came racing forward to survey the situation as the horror of a terrible mistake was revealed. The illumination round painted a clear picture of what had happened—we had been in a firefight with one of our own positions from the 1st Platoon. We stared at the other men in the position, and they looked back at us in disbelief. A medic was summoned to give aid to an unconscious GI who lay in the grass with a severe head wound. The answers were quickly falling into place. Our CO had set up a heart-shaped perimeter. Our position and the one we had engaged were situated on the two inner curves of the valentine-shaped perimeter, staring into each other's field of fire. Sergeant Bill Tanner had initiated the problem when he walked out in front of his position to defecate, instead of moving to the rear as he should have. He was the "enemy movement." Tanner had paid dearly for his mistake—he now lay in the grass, bleeding profusely from the grenade shrapnel, which had blown off half of his jaw. The other position had not known we lay to their front, and when I threw the grenade, they returned fire with their rifles and a grenade launcher. Our platoon also suffered a casualty when one of the M79 grenade rounds slammed into a case of C rations near our platoon CP. Joe Beckley received a butt full of shrapnel and was evacuated to the 22nd Surgical Hospital along with Sergeant Tanner.

After a dust-off evacuated the wounded, we nervously settled down to wait on the morning. None of us could sleep. We lay in the grass and kept company with our own thoughts and emotions. Less than an hour had passed when we were startled by a loud buzzing and bright-pink tracers soaring less than two feet above the grave mounds we crouched behind. A deafening explosion followed; then two more projectiles flew by on the same path as the first. Two or three VC were firing RPG rockets at us from a nearby tree line. They had obviously watched our small firefight and chosen to get in their two-cents' worth before vanishing into the darkness. We lay still in the dew-covered grass and dared not fire back at the enemy soldiers. They were surely scanning the graveyard for muzzle flashes, itching to fire a rocket at anyone foolish enough to give his position away. The rockets had no effect except to fray our nerves a little more and verify the fact that no one would get any sleep for the remainder of the night.

To our relief, dawn chased away the night, and we slowly uncoiled from the nests we had made in the tall, wet grass. We talked quietly among ourselves about the horrible events. We brewed up a cupful of coffee in a "B-3 unit" can and choked down pecan rolls and bread with jelly. That first cup of coffee and a cigarette always tasted good in the morning, especially after spending a bad night in the boonies. Many of us became addicted to the caffeine and nicotine that helped us get through the hard days and long nights of our Vietnam tour.

A few nights later we had just settled into our defensive perimeter and had started another night of pulling guard and slapping mosquitos when Tony Briley came crawling around to each position to inform us to pull in our claymores and prepare to move out. The squad leaders were summoned to the platoon CP, so I grabbed my rifle and made my way over to Lieutenant Melton's position. The other two squad leaders and I threw a poncho liner over our heads and turned on a red-lensed flashlight while the lieutenant unfolded his plastic-coated map and showed us where we were going.

Charlie Company was taking a beating near the coast and a sortie of

Hueys would fly in and take us to them. We would be making a night-time heliborne assault into a vicious firefight, so last-minute equipment checks would be necessary. I went back to inform the squad, then gathered my own gear as we saddled up. The load lifts were sorted out, and we moved silently to a nearby rice paddy to wait on a ride none of us wanted to take. Soon the distant drone of the Hueys grew louder, and our first sergeant stood in the middle of the paddy, holding up a strobe light. The 3rd Platoon would be going in on the first lift. The tension was almost unbearable. As soon as we were airborne someone lit a cigarette and passed it around for others to take a quick drag. I got an empty feeling in my stomach when I glanced through the Plexiglas nose of the chopper and watched the black horizon spit out thousands of tracers, while white and yellow explosions flashed in the dark like a distant thunderstorm. Someone was catching hell up ahead. I wondered if the other men in the chopper were as scared as I was. I didn't want to appear nervous and afraid, so I leaned over to Buddy Travino, slapped him on the back, and hollered, "Are you all right?" over the deafening drone of the engines. He turned around and nodded his head, but I could sense that every muscle in his body was taut as a bowstring.

The flight of choppers made a wide circle descending. We had a front-row seat viewing the intense battle going on below us. As we descended, flying parallel with the coastline, a covey of tracers flew up to greet us. The door-gunners opened up with their own version of RSVP.

The Hueys tilted up their noses for a landing, and we stood on the skids or crouched in the doorways in an effort to get out of the choppers before one of them was hit. Tracer rounds zipped past us as we jumped and raced blindly into the dark, our eyes and mouth filling with sand churned up by the rotors. I could hear the chatter of the M60 machine guns as the door-gunners gave us covering fire. The choppers lifted off to retrieve another load, and we moved about quickly in the dark, forming up our platoon.

The battle was raging just beyond a distant ridge of sand dunes, so we spread out on line and started the long trek. Charlie Company was engaging a battalion-sized element of North Vietnamese. A platoon of tanks and APCs were among their ranks, giving them support with their .50-caliber machine guns. The heavy machine guns could easily be recognized over the high-pitched chatter of the AKs and M16s. Suddenly the din of the ground fire was drowned out by a roar that stopped us in our tracks and sent a chill running up my spine. The Air Force's version of a flying fire-support base had just reached its battle station and cranked up its deadly arsenal. Several miniguns roared into action, and the sky rained death onto the entrenched enemy. The miniguns spit out thousands of rounds per second, and the tracers gave the appearance of an orange neon tube snaking its way from the sky and disappearing into the enemy positions below. The effect was devastating on the enemy as the miniguns chewed up the sand dunes around them. We had heard about this horrifying piece of war machinery, and there was no mistake that this was it. Nothing could deliver as much concentrated firepower as the nighttime marauder called "Puff the Magic Dragon." Puff was an old, converted Douglas AC47 that had been in action since the late 1930s. In World War II, it was called the "Gooneybird," but it had been renamed after a popular song of the sixties. Miniguns stuck from the airplane's sides like quills on a porcupine, each gun capable of churning out more than 6,000 rounds of 7.62mm slugs per minute. Being slow and highly maneuverable made it perfect for the job of close night support and also for kicking out flares for illumination.

We moved on to the sand dunes in front of us, then held up to wait on the rest of our company. Light resistance confronted us on the way, but we quickly compromised the enemy positions. The dunes were big and covered with small brush. At the top of the sprawling berms, we had an amazing view of the raging battle before us. We could see the whole village. The exploding shells and tracers put on a beautiful show for us, even though we knew their mere existence stood for death and suffering. The remaining two platoons soon joined us, and we were ordered to dig in on top of the dunes to serve as a blocking force. This was fine with us, and there was none of the usual complaining about digging a foxhole. The battle went on until dawn, and we fought small skirmishes all up and down our defensive line as the enemy tried to break through and escape. Several positions claimed three and four confirmed kills.

The next day we took over the task of pushing into the village. We were surprised at the continued resistance of the NVA—although they had suffered greatly from the twenty-four-hour battle, they continued to hold their ground, fighting desperately for every hedgerow. Alpha's only casualty came when a cherry was shot in the throat and died almost instantly. I felt somewhat responsible for his death, since he had been assigned initially to my squad and had served with us until just a few days before. A young teenage soldier with red hair and freckles, he had been well liked by all of us because of his easygoing personality. He had been in our squad for only a week when Lieutenant Melton instructed me to choose one man to be assigned to a squad in the 2nd Platoon, which was desperately understrength. Choosing one of my squad members had been a difficult decision, but the cherry had been my only choice, since the other men had been with us for at least two months. It had been hard to break the news to him, for we were a close-knit group who valued each other's friendship and trusted each other in combat. He hadn't wanted to leave, but I had assured him everything would be all right. He had talked privately with me about not wanting to go: "I'll go," he had said, "but something tells me not to." Now, a few days later, he was dead. I'll always remember the drained feeling I had when I realized he was the one rolled up in the poncho, being loaded onto the dust-off.

The fighting for the rest of the day was sporadic. We spent our second sleepless night as the NVA made a final attempt to push through our positions. Their numbers were drastically less than what Charlie Company had dealt with, but there was still a lot of fight left in those tough enemy soldiers. They gave us a going-over in a last-ditch effort to break through our lines. By morning their numbers were scattered, and we spent the first half of the day cleaning up the few remaining pockets of resistance.

When the battle was over, our exhaustion point had reached its peak. We were in dire need of rest and sleep, and were beginning to fight and argue with each other. Ken Fryer and Buddy Travino, the best of friends, were fighting like a cat and dog over a can of fruit cocktail. It took our whole squad to separate them.

Our CO was as tired as we were. Happily, his request to battalion headquarters for a rest earned us a two-hour break before pushing on to our night defensive location. We all dropped where we were and slept soundly, without worrying about posting guards. At that point we figured that the few enemy soldiers who might still be in the area were as tired as we and would also be looking for a place to curl up and sleep.

In two hours, Lieutenant Melton came around, kicking boots and waking us up. We would be moving out in fifteen minutes. After a quick cup of coffee and can of C's, we saddled up and moved away from the village toward another small hamlet near the beach. We had been moving nearly an hour when someone asked where Sergeant Gray was. He was a "cherry" buck sergeant just arrived from the States, who was quickly earning the reputation of being somewhat lazy and irresponsible. No one had seen him since we stopped for our break, so we concluded that he was still back in the village. We had to stop the entire company while Joey Miller took his squad back to look for him. After nearly an hour, Joey radioed that Sergeant Gray had been found and was OK. He had walked around behind a hootch and gone to sleep without letting anyone in our platoon know where he was. When we moved out, still half asleep, we had not thought to take a head count.

The next day we were somewhat rested, but it had been awfully hard on all of us to pull normal shifts of guard during the night. Men were falling asleep on guard duty, but no disciplinary action was taken. Although sleeping on guard duty was a major offense, our officers understood that we had simply been pushed beyond the limit. Over the past few months, many a nodding soldier had been rudely wakened by a slap on the head or a stinging tongue-lashing in front of his comrades after being caught asleep at his post.

That morning brought news that Alpha Company was being extracted from the boonies and sent to a naval installation on the coast for a few days of rest. The small naval fuel depot was located on the northern tip of Vinh Loc Island, which had been created centuries ago when the salty waters of the Gulf of Tonkin had surged in behind the high dunes and formed an island more than twenty miles long. The Navy had a busy schedule and required infantry soldiers to man the perimeter bunkers and conduct ambush patrols beyond the neighboring villages in order to keep the VC from running sabotage raids on the massive storage tanks and fuel bladders.

The sailors had named their camp Colco Island, but we quickly dubbed it "Cocoa Beach," which seemed to have a better sound. The navy personnel were extremely hospitable and made every effort to make us feel at home by extending their friendship and opening up their camp to us. The first day we arrived at the sleepy little naval base, we were extremely tired from our forty-eight-hour battle, and looked like something the tide had washed up. Strung out in a long column, we slowly entered the camp through the south gate and trudged along the sandy road that led past the sailor's quarters. They came out of their hootches to stare at the bedraggled column of line doggies. One of the navy men noticed the large tear in my jungle fatigue pants, ripped from one knee all the way up the crotch and over to the other knee—in desperation, I had sewn them up with stiff commo wire. I was touched when the sailor came up and handed me a pair of his own fatigue pants, assuring me he had several. I thanked him and shook his hand.

Their commanding officer ordered that the mess hall be opened immediately, but informed us to go easy on the hot chow because they were throwing a cookout for us later in the evening—steaks and beer, all we could consume, would be served on the beach. Hot showers and new fatigues were next on our schedule. It seemed the navy personnel could not do enough for us. No one complained and everyone indulged as reality slowly convinced us that this was not a dream. I couldn't help but think there was one main reason those sailors were bending over backwards for us: they were so thankful to be where they were and not in the places we had been, and would soon return to.

After the cookout on the beach, half of our company was assigned to bunker guard and ambush patrol; the other half received the night off. A movie would soon be showing against the mess-hall wall, and there were also clubs for the officers, NCOs, and enlisted men. Most of us chose to skip the movie and go to one of the three buildings that offered taped music, alcoholic beverages, and an abundance of loud talk and laughter. The "Acey-Deucey Club" was strictly for non-coms. Between the Army and Navy, it was soon overflowing with sergeants of all grades. Everyone bellied up to the bar to name their poison. Before long someone had started a beer-chugging contest; loud shouting and back-slapping cheered on the contestants as they sucked the foamy brew from aluminum cans. I was standing near the bar talking to a friend when the sharp clanging of a big brass bell brought the din of the crowd to a loud roar. Everyone turned toward the door, applauding and cheering as Bud Dykes walked in with his jungle hat resting cockily on the back of his head. Bud stood there in total ignorance and jokingly checked his fly to see if it was unbuttoned. His face slowly turned a deep shade of magenta as he tried to figure out why the crowd was making such a big issue out of his entry into the club. Then the bartender pointed to a large, hand-painted sign hanging over the bar that read, "He who wears his hat in here, will buy the bar a round of cheer!" Bud quickly reached up and snatched his flop hat from his head as though he hoped no one had seen it. He soon was laughing with the rest of us as he pulled a roll of MPCs from his pocket and shouted, "Okay! Okay! Set 'em up!"

Loud music, dirty jokes, laughter, and war stories helped the hours pass while the sailors and GIs drowned their fears and loneliness in countless mixed drinks and cans of beer. Bud and I were amused at the antics of Van Long, who would stick his head in the back door and motion for one of us to come over and bring him a beer. He was not allowed in the club because of his rank, so Bud and I kept a beer in his hand the entire night by paying for a couple, then stepping outside as though we were going to visit the urinal. He sat outside the back door of the club, slowly sipping cold beer and listening to the twangy Vietnamese music on his pocket-sized transistor radio.

It was sometime after midnight when shouts and roaring laughter gained everyone's attention. Half the men in the clubhouse raced out the rear screen door to investigate. There, standing up to his chest in a fifty-five-gallon steel drum, was Sgt. Jerry Piester from the 1st Platoon. Both ends of the steel drum had been cut out and it had been sunk into the ground with only a couple of inches protruding from the soft, white sand. A screen mesh had been strapped over the open barrel, and it had been half filled with kerosene. The drum was used as a urinal, and it was now filled to the top with a potent mixture of fuel oil and urine. Jerry was in no condition to be wandering around in the dark by himself, and while looking for the urinal he had tripped over the protruding rim of the drum and fallen, with a splash, through the screen. No one wanted to get near him, so he slowly crawled from the barrel and made his way toward the surf to bathe in the ocean. One of his buddies brought him a bar of soap, and he stayed in the warm surf bathing for more than an hour; his boots and clothes washed out to sea. It was an incident we would laugh about for a long time. The Navy made the best of it too. The next day we discovered a freshly painted sign by the urinal: "Piester's Pisser."

Our second day at Cocoa found most of our platoon pulling bunker guard while others prepared for an ambush about a mile south of the camp. My squad was one of the elements assigned to the ambush patrol. We were somewhat nervous due to the unfamiliar terrain and the report of numerous VC within the area. We conducted our patrol as usual and had negative contact. We encountered only one problem—nearly all of us became deathly sick with stomach cramps and diarrhea during the night. It must have been from all of the rich food and alcohol we had consumed within the past twenty-four hours. Our bodies had grown used to 3 modest meals of C rations washed down with water highly tainted with iodine tablets; our digestive systems were just not used to good, wholesome food, especially in such gluttonous quantities. Diarrhea was something to which we had grown accustomed, but this sudden siege sapped our strength. It was a good thing no contact was made that night, for none of us were in any condition to do battle with the enemy. The entire night was spent lying in the brush, then crawling off a short distance to relieve the gut-grinding sickness that churned within us.

About halfway through the night, I had used up a pocket full of small toilet paper packets, which we all collected from C-ration boxes. I quietly removed my fatigue shirt and pulled my OD T-shirt from my back. (T-shirts were the only thing in the underwear category that most of us wore, since we had stopped wearing skivvy shorts long before.) I sat in the dark with a pocket knife and cut the T-shirt into neat little squares, which served me well for the rest of the night. Morning found us hurrying back to camp in search of medics who would help our condition by rationing out doses of a foul, chalky liquid that closed down our intestinal tracts like a locked door.

By nighttime most of us had recovered, and back we went to the Acey-Deucey Club for another rowdy evening of singing along with the loud music and drowning our thoughts in the inexhaustible supplies of alcoholic beverages. I left the club about midnight and crashed on an old, broken-down army cot. Having been asleep for less than an hour, I was awakened by a sergeant from another platoon who informed me that Bud had drunk himself beyond control and was running naked around the camp. He had taken a swing at a couple of GIs who had tried to help him, and now they had come to me since I was his best friend. Our main concern was to find him before he wandered beyond the bunker line and was possibly mistaken for an enemy soldier and fired upon. With the help of five or six soldiers and sailors, I found him running stark naked in the moonlit surf. He was beyond reason, so I tackled him in the wet sand and lifted him onto my shoulder in the traditional "fireman's carry." I had carried him for two or three hundred yards when the constant pressure of my shoulder in his stomach led to an extremely unpleasant event: without warning, Bud raised his head and threw up down my back from neck to boots. My first thought was to drown him, but the laughter from the other men made me realize how funny it really must have looked. I unloaded Bud, and immediately stripped and waded into the surf to wash my clothes, just as Sergeant Piester had done two nights before.

When Bud sobered up the next morning and learned what he had done, he apologized to me for more than an hour. I simply laughed it off —it was just one of the crazy things that had happened during our first stay at Cocoa Beach. That night, quite unintentionally, I had a chance to pay back Bud for his escapade.

Our platoon had been assigned to man the positions at the southern perimeter line: the huge bunkers the Navy had built were manned by six to eight GIs. Shortly after dark, I let four of our men, Bud among them, walk back into camp to see the movie. It was shown out in the open, with the audience sitting in the sand or propped up against one of the many pine trees that dotted the camp. I was positioned at the beachside bunker overlooking the surf. It was topped off by a .50-caliber machine gun and several cases of ammunition. We sat on top of the bunker and enjoyed the warm ocean breeze, talking quietly to each other about girlfriends, families, and home. Everything was quiet, and the monotony of the waves rolling up on the beach turned our thoughts toward dreaming up some form of entertainment. Ken Fryer mentioned that he had always wanted to fire the .50 caliber, since not too many line doggies ever got the chance to crank up one of those death-dealing weapons. We all agreed it would be fun to watch the tracers dance off the Gulf of Tonkin, so I radioed our company CP: "The South perimeter is about to test fire its machine guns." There was no objection to our request, so we took turns blowing holes in the moonlit water with several hundred ball and tracer rounds from the heavy machine gun. Everyone took a turn with the gun, and then we settled back to continue our chores of guarding the perimeter.

A few minutes later Bud and the other three movie-watchers came charging up with their rifles at the ready, shouting, "Where are they? Are they inside the wire?" We looked at them as though they were crazy. Then it dawned on us—they thought the bunker line was under attack and that their help was urgently needed. The firing had created havoc among the moviegoers, because the four of them had stepped all over everyone as they raced to our assistance. While they gasped for breath, we laughed at the joke we had innocently played on them. Then I walked over to Bud and assured him that now we were even!

The next morning brought the sad news that we would be boarding choppers within the next two hours and flying back to Eight-Klick Ville. Delta Company was flying in to relieve us at Cocoa, and it was our turn to go back to the boonies and deal with the VC and NVA.

Cocoa Beach was a place we would visit several times within the next few months, since the Army realized its troops must have an occasional break from guerrilla warfare. It had been an enjoyable three days, and we had been able to vent some of the anger and tension that were bottled up inside us. Our batteries were recharged and we were ready to go back and face the hell that Eight Klick was sure to deal out.

As we prepared to leave, Van Long came over to Bud and me and jabbered in broken English, "Cocoa Beach numba one! Eight Klick numba ten!" He had learned to speak English pretty well and had become an invaluable asset to our company. A warm friendship had grown between the three of us over the past few weeks. We felt a responsibility to help take care of Van Long by preventing any of the other GIs from teasing him or pushing him around. Whenever possible, Van Long stayed with our platoon simply to be close to Bud and me.

Eight-Klick Ville welcomed us back by mangling the feet of Sp4 Brad Allen when he stepped on a booby trap less than thirty minutes after our return. The relaxed feeling we had experienced at Cocoa Beach vanished. Then a lone VC fired several poorly aimed rounds at us from a confiscated M79 grenade launcher. He had obviously taken the American-made weapon from the body of a dead GI or ARVN and was satisfied to hide in the brush and fire blindly at us from about 200 yards away. The next couple of days were spent trying to avoid stepping on land mines and coping with the lone snipers that constantly harassed us.

One evening, just after we had set up our defensive perimeter, Lieutenant Melton informed me I would be taking an ambush into the heart of "bad country." The CO wanted to brief me on the location, so the lieutenant and I walked over to the company CP and Captain Keever unfolded his map to point out our ambush site with a red-lens flashlight. He was somewhat hesitant about showing me exactly where battalion headquarters had ordered an ambush patrol. I was appalled at their decision, for it was one of the most heavily booby-trapped and VC-infested spots in the entire area. It would have been bad enough taking a patrol in there during the day, but a night patrol was definitely suicidal. When I questioned the orders, the captain confirmed them—in a tone of voice that assured me of his own fear for the treacherous village. I looked again at the map and instantly came to a decision: I would take my squad on ambush patrol, but would not lead them into that particular section of Eight Klick just to satisfy some captain sitting behind a map at LZ Sally. I informed Captain Keever and Lieutenant Melton that I was not going into the village and that they would have to come up with another ambush site before I would take out my squad. Lieutenant Melton threw a quick glance my way, and although he said nothing, I could tell he was in total agreement with me. I also felt that the CO wanted to cancel the patrol, but he again informed me that I would have to take the ambush into that area, since he could not go against orders from battalion. With as much tact and respect as I could muster, I again told him, "No!" This time he accepted my refusal and firmly, but with understanding, directed me to another ambush site. I accepted the alternate location and walked away to inform the squad, feeling badly about having to disobey a direct order. This was a first for me, but I felt very strongly about my decision and had made up my mind to stick with it.

As we prepared our gear to move out, Lieutenant Melton came over and made a recheck to be sure I knew the location of our new ambush site. He also told me that a cherry buck sergeant from the 2nd Platoon had volunteered to take his squad into the village, to the ambush site I had refused. I remember feeling sorry for his men, not for him, since they, as veterans of Eight Klick, knew what to expect, and he did not. Before leaving the perimeter, I checked with Papa One, our FO, and coordinated the grids for calling in artillery in case it was needed. I crawled into the harness of the PRC-25 and motioned the squad to form up. Everyone fell into place with weapons at the ready, flop hat and camo grease in place, and claymores and bandoliers of machine-gun ammunition draped over the shoulders. They were all seasoned veterans —professionals who knew how to do their jobs. I felt proud to be with them, yet ashamed to let them know I had refused a direct order from our commanding officer. I never told anyone about my confrontation with Captain Keever, not even my best friend Bud. A few weeks later I found out I had been up for a promotion to staff sergeant (E-6), but my orders were pulled because of the incident over the ambush patrol.

We were mere shadows in the dark as we slipped quietly through the perimeter and headed toward our destination nearly a mile away. An overcast sky made the night as black as a cave, so I chose to stay in the open and take the long route, leading us across a vast area of rice paddies. The short route would have led us down the edge of Eight Klick, where we would be subject to bumping into VC patrols or walking blindly into a field of booby traps and land mines. A small compass was our only guide as we slowly made our way across the sun-dried paddies and dikes. Our first checkpoint would be an islandlike hamlet standing by itself in the center of a large paddy. Three or four hootches lay in this oasis of bamboo, which we had seen from a distance but had never taken time to search. A faint orange glow from a lantern told us we were drawing close to the oasis, so we crouched behind a nearby dike to listen for signs of activity. We spread out and crawled on our bellies to the edge of the hamlet. Lying under the cover of a bamboo thicket, we could hear several male voices chattering excitedly in one of the hootches. I whispered to Bud that we needed a closer look, so the two of us crawled like snakes to within a few feet of the hootch. Thick vegetation and darkness prevented us from getting a good look, but we did hear the voices of women and children. We decided to leave them alone and not take the chance of being detected.

We silently made our way back to the waiting squad and led them off into the darkness toward our destination. Another hour of carefully picking our way across the rice stubble found us near the trail where we were to set up our ambush. I sent out Ric and Buddy to scout the area while I called the CP and gave them a sitrep. Upon the scouts' return we moved into the site and settled down behind a large dike. Our kill zone consisted of a well-used trail that came across the rice paddies and made a fork just before entering the hamlets of Eight Klick. Ambush reports from other companies working in the area indicated that the VC often used this trail. There we were, waiting in the dark on anyone who might come along.

The line doggie had many duties he abhorred; probably the one most impersonal and disliked was the night ambush patrol. Nighttime ambushes were designed to be quick and deadly, with the result being total annihilation of everything in the kill zone. The participants in the mortal game of ambush had the advantage of lying in the darkness with a deadly arsenal of automatic rifles, machine guns, and claymore mines. The victims, who might be NVA soldiers, Viet Cong, innocent civilians, or stray dogs, were caught up in a fatal blast of lead and steel that abruptly ended their journey. Not all ambush patrols were successful. The majority were uneventful; some were "rolled up" by the crafty enemy soldiers, with the GIs suffering casualties or having to flee in the night—having been transformed from "hunter" to "hunted."

We had settled into our ambush and were pulling 50 percent guard when a sudden burst of automatic-rifle fire erupted from within the depths of Eight Klick. I reached for the radio receiver and listened intently for a message I hoped would not come. The firing was nearly a mile away and was coming from the area where I was initially ordered to take my squad. In less than a minute, the panic-stricken voice of the cherry buck sergeant barked over the radio that their patrol had been hit. I could tell that fear was about to overtake him, since his transmission was broken and confusing. As his lieutenant tried to calm him on the other end of the radio, I pressed the receiver to my ear to listen. The young and inexperienced squad leader called for help, shouting that several members of his squad were dead or wounded. I lay there with mixed emotions, realizing I could have easily been in his place. I found myself mumbling words that had become common among the line doggies—"Better him than me!"

Hours passed as we lay motionless in the dark. Mike Brinson left his machine gun for a moment and crawled over to me to point out movement, barely visible against a distant tree line. He instructed me to stare at three or four parachute flares slowly drifting earthward in the far-off sky. Their faint light was just enough to outline the silhouettes of soldiers, stretched out in a long column nearly a hundred yards to our right flank. As more distant flares blossomed in the sky, we realized there were definitely more troops than we could take on. Mike and I crawled around our small perimeter and informed the rest of our squad of the troop movement. We couldn't tell if they were friend or foe, so I called the CP and asked if there were any friendly elements near our patrol site. The answer was negative. I then told them of the massive column of troops crossing the wide rice paddy. I asked for artillery fire to be brought in on the enemy soldiers, but was informed that it could not be done without positive identification. Cursing into the radio, I again gave our FO the facts: the entire squad had seen the movement, and we estimated their numbers to be from one to two hundred. Frustration sickened me as once again we were stopped short of dealing a heavy blow to the enemy by political procedures, ordered by an unknown staff of officers manning their charts and maps in the safety of some far-off base camp. The troop movement soon disappeared, but the mere thought of their presence forced us into pulling 100 percent alert for the rest of the night.

As dawn terminated our ambush patrol, we gathered in the claymores and slowly made our way back to the company perimeter. Rejoining the platoon, we learned that the other ambush patrol had been hit hard as they moved into the center of the VC-infested village. They had obviously been detected as they entered the hamlet, for a squad of VC ambushed them as they made their way along the darkened trails. Their casualties were not as numerous as the cherry squad leader had originally stated over the radio, but they had received one KIA. One seasoned member of the squad had been shot through the head, and another suffered a minor flesh wound in the leg.

As I made my way to the company CP to report the details of the troop movement to Captain Keever, I noticed the cherry buck sergeant sitting on a small grave mound with a forlorn expression on his face. He looked up at me as I approached, but quickly turned his head as our eyes met. Although I felt sorry for him, I knew there was no place for pity in this incident. He had made a grave mistake while trying to be a hero, and it had cost the life of a Screaming Eagle.

I gave my report to the CO, and he again tried to explain why I had not received artillery on the detected troop movement. Our respect for one another was already frayed, so I accepted his explanation as though I totally understood. He ordered me to take a four-man LP back to the ambush area and remain there for most of the day. Our mission would be to give the company advance warning of concentrated enemy movement, since Alpha Company would be breaking up into platoons and conducting search-and-clear missions throughout the small villages.

Ric, Bud, Tony, and I packed up our gear and prepared to leave the company area as the morning sun quickly heated the still, humid air. We reached our destination by mid morning and hastily found a thick cluster of shrub and bamboo that overlooked a wide area in three directions. To our front lay a marsh crisscrossed with trails; to our right and left flank lay vast fields of recently harvested rice. We sat quietly in the shade and puffed on crooked cigarettes that Ric extracted from a crushed pack on which he had slept.

As we murmured softly to each other, mostly about trivial memories of home, a loud, metallic sound gained our attention and sent four rifle safeties clicking to the "auto" position. Staring out from under our thick cover, we watched a half-naked VC walk out of the distant tree line and stand on the edge of the marsh as though scouting the area for possible danger. He was less than a hundred yards away, and we could see the AK47 slung over his shoulder and the iron cooking pot hanging heavily from his left hand. All four of us had a bead on him, ready to squeeze the trigger at the slightest suggestion that he had detected us.

He stood there for at least a minute. A smile was forced to our faces as we watched him pick his nose and wipe his finger on a tree. Then he turned, shouted a few words into the tree line, and began to move back. Now that we knew the VC was not alone, we decided to try to surprise the entire group. I radioed Lieutenant Melton and asked him to stand by with the platoon for possible assistance. I instructed Tony and Ric to stay hidden with the radio while Bud and I moved into the village. We left our heavy gear with Ric and Tony, each of us taking nothing but our rifle and a bandolier of ammo wrapped around our waist.

Crawling silently through the brush, I could feel a cold sweat begin to moisten my clothes; one look at Bud assured me he was just as tense as I. Reaching the spot where we had seen the VC, we paused to look and listen for signs of him and his comrades. Everything was still and quiet, so we crept on into the village, ready to cut down anything that moved. Finding no signs of the VC patrol, we made our way back to where Ric and Tony were anxiously waiting. They informed us that Lieutenant Melton was leading the platoon in our direction to help us flush out the enemy soldiers. When they found us nearly an hour later, we studied our maps and figured out a way to surround the hamlet in hopes that the VC were still around. My guess was that they had moved deeper into the village where Bud and I had not searched. If they had stopped to prepare a meal, our chances of catching them off guard were very good.

We broke up into squads and moved out in three different directions with the intention of rendezvousing on the opposite side of the village. As our squad cautiously made its way through the trails and hootches, the sudden chatter of rifle fire told us contact had been made. Joey Miller's squad, sweeping the left flank, had obviously spooked the small patrol of VC—they caught a glimpse of them disappearing into a distant tree line. Several men had opened up on the fleeing enemy, but managed only to kick up dust at the edge of the trees. We called in a Huey for aerial surveillance, but the elusive enemy had vanished, unscathed, and would have another chance at us whenever the opportunity arose.

Eight-Klick Ville continued to plague us as we snared the trip wires of booby traps and served as targets for invisible snipers. Humping the boonies around Eight Klick was like playing Russian roulette with five out of six cylinders loaded instead of the traditional five out of six empty. Each step was a gamble, and many soldiers paid the price—a severed foot, mangled legs, or a gut full of hot shrapnel. Days had passed since we left Cocoa, and the dreadful conditions of Eight Klick had once again turned us into nervous, high-strung foot soldiers. Every day, we fought the battle of trying to maintain our sanity while coaxing the invisible enemy into engaging us rather than evading us like shadows in the twilight.

A new first sergeant had recently been assigned to our company, and for the first time in months we were experiencing the services of a "top sergeant" in the field instead of from our base camp. First Sergeant Andrew Soward was a fellow North Carolinian. He won the respect of the entire company by spending most of his time in the boonies instead of trying to handle the many problems of Alpha Company from LZ Sally. He was an easygoing individual, unlike any first sergeant we had known, but he ran our company with a firm hand.

After spending several days with us in Eight Klick, First Sergeant Soward went back to LZ Sally to take care of the growing stacks of administrative papers. Before flying out on an LOH, he gave Sergeant First Class Hands the responsibility of "acting first sergeant." Eddie Hands would run our company during the first sergeant's absence, giving him the multiple duties of platoon sergeant and first sergeant. One major chore he inherited was coordinating the log ship, which brought in our daily supplies of mail, food, ammo, and equipment. This process took about an hour and a half and normally fell into the hands of the first sergeant or some other ranking NCO. Unless we were engaged in a firefight or were in extremely dangerous territory, taking "log" was a time to relax and vent the tension we had stored away.

One afternoon Sergeant Hands was carrying out the log chores with his usual professionalism; he had called in a "de-log" Huey, after distributing all of the loot the chopper had brought in nearly an hour earlier. Everything was running smoothly as his detail of privates hustled about, loading the empty water cans and mailbags onto the Huey that had squatted down on a nearby sun-baked paddy. The platoon leaders and their squad leaders huddled in small groups, discussing the orders for our night patrols and perimeter location. We then moved back to our squads to brief them and wait on the concealing shadows of dusk before moving out. As we savored the day's last cigarettes and relaxed in the long shadows of the late afternoon sun, a lone Viet Cong was patiently waiting nearby for us to walk into his deadly trap.

Sergeant Hands' company duties were now complete, so he rejoined our platoon. "Pick 'em up and move out," was transmitted over the radios, with the order of movement putting the Third Herd in the lead. My squad would walk point, so we formed up and began the move to our night defensive location, which lay nearly a mile away. Lieutenant Melton was up front with us while Eddie Hands took up his usual position at the rear of the platoon along with his RTO and a 90mm recoilless-rifle team. Movement was slow and deliberate as we carefully picked our way along the winding trail that skirted the edge of Eight Klick. There was little talk as everyone's attention was focused on the ground to his front in search of trip wires or suspicious mounds of dirt, which might conceal a land mine. We had gone only a few yards when the hopes of an uneventful night were suddenly shattered—a tremendous explosion belched from behind us and threw us hard against the dusty earth. I had never before been so close to such a horrific blast. The concussion alone slammed against my back as though I had been run over by a truck. Tree limbs, dirt, rocks, and choking dust rained down on us for what seemed like an eternity as we lay in the brush and covered our heads and faces with our hands. When the dust began to settle, each GI slowly lifted his head to see if the buddy who had been at his side a moment earlier was still there. As I wiped the dirt from my eyes I caught a glimpse of Bud and Ric cautiously crawling out of a bomb crater where they had been thrown. Others slowly climbed to their knees, gazing around in disbelief that any of us were still alive. As Lieutenant Melton ordered us to fan out and set up security, a sharp cry for a medic sent a chill up my spine. The blast had occurred within our platoon, and we would have to wait for several minutes before learning the extent of our casualties. As we lay in the fading light and listened to the distant drone of an approaching dust-off, Lieutenant Melton came forward to our positions. His eyes were moist with tears. Disbelief surged through me as the lieutenant dropped his head and uttered, "It's Sergeant Hands."

I started to rise, to race back to where the explosion had taken place, but Lieutenant Melton stopped me; he said I would be better off staying with the squad rather than seeing the mangled body of our fallen friend. We were devastated and simply couldn't accept the fact that Eddie Hands was dead. Sergeant Hands had been standing beside a small bunker when he suddenly disappeared in a ball of yellow and orange flame. His body was thrown backward nearly a hundred yards and landed in the midst of the 2nd Platoon. They had carefully wrapped him in a poncho and stayed with his body while medics treated the other wounded GIs. Miraculously no one else suffered severe wounds from the giant blast. The radio operator for Sergeant Hands had a broken collarbone and lacerations, and two men from the 90mm team had ruptured eardrums.

Just as the dust-off lumbered in to pick up the casualties, we started receiving well-aimed rounds from one or two M79 grenade launchers. The shells fell heavily near the churning Huey while it was being loaded. The VC were adding insult to injury, and the entire company turned their weapons toward the origin of the incoming fire. The mad firing continued for nearly five minutes, and the nearby hamlet was practically leveled. Our officers let us continue firing, realizing we needed to release some of the anger burning within us. After Eddie Hands's body was extracted with the wounded, we moved on to our night defensive location with the intention of returning the next morning to search for clues as to what had caused the fatal blast.

At dawn we began the long trek back to the previous evening's log site, anxious to find out what type of explosive device the VC had used against us. Reaching our destination, a wide perimeter was established around the site, and we began sifting through the scattered debris. Digging through the crater, we found the tail fins of a 250-pound aerial bomb that was part of the arsenal of our air force fighter-bombers. Obviously the bomb had not detonated when it was dropped from one of our jets. The VC had buried it in a bunker along a well-used path. The bomb had also been "command-detonated"—we found a half-buried stretch of commo wire leading away from the crater to a well-concealed hiding place in a nearby line of trees. All the puzzle pieces were falling into place: some crafty Viet Cong had watched Sergeant Hands conduct his logging responsibilities and guessed him to be one of our honchos. The VC had patiently waited for the right moment to squeeze off the claymore detonator we found attached to the other end of the wire. Our entire platoon had walked past the bunker that was holding the giant bomb; the explosion had occurred when Eddie Hands was practically on top of it.

As we continued our search, a private beckoned several of us over to a thicket where he stood holding some unrecognizable object. I detected a sick look on his face as he held out the object without saying a word. There, in his hands, was the left arm of our platoon sergeant, which still bore his wedding band on a swollen finger. I felt like throwing up, but simply choked back the lump in my throat, turned, and walked away.

Someone wrapped the arm in a poncho and tagged it so it could be sent back to LZ Sally and reunited with the body.

Much to our chagrin, we were ordered to stay in the general area for the next several days and continue searching and clearing the hamlets, which were now totally deserted by the civilian population. The 2nd Platoon suffered heavy casualties on one particular clearing operation. They suddenly found themselves in the center of a brushy area impregnated with bouncing Betty land mines. These were the Soviet version of the well-known antipersonnel mine, which, when triggered, would spring upward and explode about head high. One mine could take out an entire squad. Before our 2nd Platoon could drag their dead and wounded from the mine field, nearly half of them were members of a bloody casualty list. The platoon was so understrength that the CO decided to send over some men from 1st and 3rd to build up the squads until replacements arrived: I was one of those temporarily assigned. I was very reluctant to be a squad leader with men I didn't know well, but deep inside, I knew the real reason was not wanting to leave the friends and buddies to whom I had grown so close over the past several months.

I moved to the 2nd Platoon and took over one of the squads that had been drastically decreased in size by the land-mine incident. Within two days, five green cherries had been assigned to the squad, which made us one of the most uncoordinated and inefficient elements in the entire battalion. Only three of us in the squad had any combat experience, and we spent most of our time trying to shape up the new recruits so they would not pose a danger to themselves and to us. Regardless of the warnings we gave them, they didn't realize just how treacherous Eight Klick could be until one afternoon they were brought face-to-face with stark reality.

We were searching a small hamlet over grown with bamboo thickets and tall grass; movement through the brush was slow and dangerous. Our squad had spread out on line and was picking its way through the hootches and bunkers when a nearby explosion sent us all clamoring for safety. Racing over to the explosion site, I found one of the cherries and one of the seasoned vets sprawled facedown in a low-lying marshy area. They had been trying to cross a shallow water-filled trench when one of them had triggered a land mine. Two medics ran over to help as I pulled the moaning cherry from the mud and rolled him on his back. He was the most critically injured of the two. I placed his head on my knees to keep him from choking on the blood surging from his mouth and from a large hole in his chin. How he remained conscious, I'll never know, for his body was perforated with dozens of gaping holes; blood poured out of them, forming small puddles on the sticky, black soil. The medics worked hard at trying to stop the bleeding, while I cradled his head in my lap and held an IV bottle above him. The young soldier fought for his life as blood continued to spill from his body. As he got weaker and weaker, he made one last attempt to raise his head and speak. A cough gurgled from his lips and he looked squarely into my eyes and pleaded, "Don't let me die in this mud." I held his muddy hand and tried to convince him he would be all right and would soon be receiving excellent medical attention at the 22nd Surg, in Phu Bai. The medics continued to work over him, but he drifted into unconsciousness and died before a dust-off arrived.

I was emotionally drained, feeling as though I had let him down. A sudden rush of anguish, fatigue, frustration, and anger surged over me. I broke down and cried like a small child, still holding his head, which had just been covered by his bloody fatigue jacket.

In less than two weeks I was back with my old squad in the 3rd Platoon. Bud had been squad leader in my absence and had proven himself once again while on ambush patrol in a VC-infested hamlet. He had taken the squad out in search of small Viet Cong elements known to move about freely in one particular area of Eight Klick. While sneaking through a cluster of deserted hootches, they spotted enemy movement and immediately went into a defensive position. Somehow, they were detected and drew heavy fire from the VC patrol, which turned out to be larger than they had at first estimated. Pinned down and unable to maneuver on the VC, the squad lay in the thick undergrowth and returned fire that effectively held the enemy at bay. Seeing the predicament they were in, Bud left the squad and crawled away, by himself, working his way around behind the enemy gunners; he then charged into them and scattered their positions by killing five and capturing two. Not a single GI had been hurt. Because of his heroic efforts, Bud was later awarded the Silver Star.

It was good to be back with my old friends in the Third Herd, though I had become close to the men in the 2nd Platoon. My first night back would be one many of us would never forget. Lieutenant Melton brought the squad leaders together late in the afternoon and briefed us on an ambush site to which the entire platoon would be moving as soon as darkness fell. We prepared our gear, stacked our rucksacks at the company CP so we could travel lightly, and then set out just before dark. The ambush site lay nearly a mile away, and our journey would lead us through stagnant marshes and vast fields of harvested rice. As we made our way around a large rice paddy, we detected three enemy soldiers hurrying across the dikes on the far side of the flat, dry field. They were barely recognizable as the last rays of light slipped below the horizon. They were too far away, and firing into them would only jeopardize our mission, so we chose to let them pass.

An hour later we reached our ambush site and moved in silently to secure the area. We were to ambush an intersection of two large trails, with my squad taking the right flank while Joey Miller's squad took rear security; another took the left flank. The positions had been determined before we left the company perimeter, so very few instructions were needed as the well-seasoned GIs moved silently into place. Lieutenant Melton walked over and whispered that I should recheck my squad to make sure every position had set up the proper fields of fire. This was SOP on all ambush patrols, so I reached for my rifle and set out to crawl around to each position. My first checkpoint was the machine-gun team, manned by "Pete" Peterson, "Handy" Matthews, and "Junior" Deal. I crouched low and made my way over to the three of them; they were kneeling in the thick grass, busily linking together several belts of M60 ammo. Pete assured me he could cover the entire kill zone from where his gun was positioned. I turned and was moving toward the next position when a savage explosion picked me up and hurled me bodily into Lieutenant Melton's position at the rear of the ambush site. A burning sensation raced up my arm as I scrambled to my hands and knees in search of my rifle. Cries of pain filled the dark, damp night as Lieutenant Melton grabbed me and yelled, "What the hell's goin' on?" Fear and confusion took charge of our platoon when someone shouted, "Incoming mortars!" making us all scramble for cover. In less than a minute we regained our senses and realized that someone had triggered a large land mine. Several of our comrades were critically wounded. Orders were barked out for those who were okay to take up security positions while the victims were attended to. Cries for help came from all directions, and we crawled around in the dark searching for the dead and wounded. Lieutenant Melton called back to the company CP, requesting more medics and a dust-off.

As I made my way over to the area of the explosion, I stumbled over a limp body that made no gesture for help. I reached down to roll him over and someone directed the beam of a red-lensed flashlight into the face of the critically wounded soldier. It was Pete, his face and chest a solid mass of blood and torn flesh. He had been standing directly over the mine when it blew up. Pete was still alive but choking on the blood that surged from his neck wounds and filled his mouth and throat. There was only one thing to do. I buried my face in his and sucked the blood from his shattered mouth. I almost gagged at the taste of the warm, sweet liquid, but after I had removed much of it from his mouth, he began to breathe easier and give out deep, guttural moans. Doc Reems inserted an IV in his arm, stuffed gauze in his wounds, handed me the bottle, and instructed me to watch him while he checked on the others. It was then, when I lifted the IV bottle, that I noticed a trickle of blood running slowly down my arm and dripping inside my shirt. I suddenly remembered the burning in my left arm just after the explosion—I had forgotten it during the horror and excitement that followed. I reached for my left hand, which was clutching the IV bottle, and discovered that half my thumb was pointing back toward my wrist. It had been penetrated by a small piece of shrapnel and was neatly severed at the last joint. Pain began to shoot up my arm. I switched the bottle to my other hand and continued to watch over Pete.

Doc Reems recruited Lieutenant Melton and his RTO to help him with the other wounded soldiers. Junior Deal had an eye blown out and a large hole in his chest; Handy Matthews was bleeding profusely from severe lacerations in his butt and legs. Nine of us had been hit by the razor-sharp shrapnel; my broken thumb turned out to be the least serious wound of all. Suffering and carnage was all around as Uncle Sam's proud youth lay in the dark, bleeding quietly on the damp grass.

The entire 2nd Platoon soon arrived with three more medics. They had thrown all precautions to the wind and had jogged nearly a mile through the treacherous enemy terrain in order to rush to our assistance. It made me proud to see their sweaty faces in the dim light of the flashlights, for I knew they had risked their lives. They helped us salvage what was left of our crippled platoon, gathering up the wounded and the scattered gear. The distant drone of an approaching dust-off was heard. One of the men from the 2nd Platoon walked to a nearby clearing and turned on a strobe light. The medevac soon landed and all of the wounded were either led or carried to the waiting chopper. All of our weapons and equipment were left behind, since hospitals had no use for their patients' baggage and belongings. The equipment would be sent back to base camp, sorted out, and reissued to incoming cherries.

It was a long, cool ride to Phu Bai, where we would be treated in the air-conditioned emergency rooms of the 22nd Surgical Hospital. When we touched down on the helipad, dozens of medics converged on the dust-off and carefully unloaded its bloody cargo. I was the only ambulatory patient in the bunch, so I stepped aside and watched my buddies being lifted onto stretchers and rushed off to the air-bubble operating units that squatted in the dark like giant mushrooms. A medic led me through two swinging doors and into a strange environment. Bright lights hung over two long rows of operating tables; the air was cool and clean and smelled of disinfectant and medical supplies. I was told to sit in a corner until someone could take care of me. Dozens of doctors appeared from nowhere and proceeded to scrub their arms and hands. Medics went from table to table cutting every stitch of sweaty, muddy clothing from the GIs who lay flat on their backs under the glaring lights. Pete, Handy, and Junior were the most seriously wounded and each had at least three or four doctors working over their limp bodies. I sat quietly and watched as tubes and needles were jammed into their arms and catheters inserted; the doctors quickly inspected their wounds and decided what critical procedures should be taken first. I silently prayed that I would not have to witness a sheet being pulled over their faces.

As three doctors worked over Pete, he suddenly convulsed and rolled over on his side. The tubes and IV bottles swung violently as he vomited all over one of the doctors. I heard them comment that it was a good sign for him to react to nausea by leaning over and trying to throw up on the floor.

The operating room stayed busy for nearly two hours as each GI was worked on by the highly trained professional staff of the 22nd Surg. I had not yet been attended to and was still sitting quietly in the corner when someone placed a hand on my shoulder and asked, "How're you feeling, Sarge?" I turned around and was surprised to see Colonel Huntley (White Falcon), our battalion commander. He had heard about our catastrophe and had flown in to check on us. I rose and shook his extended hand, informing him as much as I could about the incident. He gazed out across the rows of operating tables that held the naked, bleeding bodies of his paratroopers. Turning around to say a few final words, I was sure I detected a glaze of tears in the corners of his eyes.

As the wounded soldiers were being wrapped in bandages, a female nurse approached me and asked me to lie down on a nearby table. No sooner had I stretched out on the cold, stainless-steel slab than she came at me with a huge pair of scissors and proceeded to cut my boots and fatigues away from my filthy body. We all smelled horribly from the stagnant marsh through which we had waded on our way to the ambush site—this first lieutenant even made a joke about me having fallen into a latrine sump. I was somewhat what uneasy about her nonchalantly cutting away my clothes and pitching them into a large garbage can, but she told me not to worry, she did this at least twenty or thirty times a day.

By the time the doctors had finished with the more seriously wounded and gotten around to me, it was well into the night. I was amazed at how fresh and in control they seemed to be. My entire arm was scrubbed and shaved before an oversized syringe was emptied into my armpit. After the anesthetic took hold, they opened up my thumb, just the way one would split a baked potato before piling in the butter and sour cream. The wound was left open in order to drain and flush out any infection that may already have taken hold. They bandaged my hand and carted me off to a dimly lit ward full of sleeping GIs wearing bandages of all shapes and sizes. I immediately fell asleep, only to wake up a couple of hours later with my left hand throbbing with pain. I summoned a ward attendant, who quickly put me at ease with another syringe—this time targeted for a spot well below my armpit. By mid morning I had traded in my swaddling sheet for a pair of pajamas and flimsy cloth slippers, and made my way toward a chow line. I hurried through breakfast so I could search out my buddies and find out how serious their wounds really were. Pete and Junior were in intensive care, scheduled to be flown to Tokyo as soon as possible, but I was able to locate the others in various wards throughout the complex.

We stayed at the 22nd Surgical Hospital for another day and were then flown by a C-130 hospital craft to the 91st Evacuation Hospital at Tui Hoa. Here, with large wards and plenty of movies and recreation areas for the patients, life was a little easier. There was nothing to do but rest and sleep, and the line doggies who filled the rows of beds took full advantage of the opportunity. The only thing I detested was having to watch the nurses and doctors change the bandages on the soldiers with the most severe wounds. Their cries of pain were too much to listen to. As soon as my hand was checked and rewrapped I would leave the ward and not return until the screams of agony had ceased.

Our third day at the 91st Evac brought news that Bob Phillips had been seen at the hospital and was in one of the wards on the far side of the hospital area. Bob was one of three RTOs our CO always had at his side. We wondered what sort of wound or sickness had brought him to Tui Hoa. A couple of us set out to find him, and in less than an hour we were hearing the frightening story of Bob's accident at LZ Sally. I listened in disbelief and horror as he told us how he had lost his right hand and had his left hand badly mangled.

Bob had taken a de-log chopper back to Sally, to have some minor dental work done. He had not been able to catch a chopper back to the boonies, so he chose to spend the night at base camp, returning to the company the next day. The accident happened as he was returning to Alpha Company's camp hootch, on his way back from the evening chow line. A young cherry lieutenant had taken it upon himself to give an informal class to a small group of cherry privates on the procedures of arming and disarming a LAW. The lieutenant had led the small class out to the bunker line and picked one of the rocket launchers from the arsenal of weapons issued to each massive bunker. He was in the process of disarming the telescopic launching tube when the rocket accidentally fired. Bob was simply strolling by and looked up just in time to see the rocket coming straight for him. Instinctively he threw up his arms to deflect the missile. It ricocheted off his hands, barely missing his head; since it had not traveled far enough to arm itself, there was no explosion. Bob was thrown to the ground by the impact, and when he tried to pick himself up, he realized he no longer had the use of his hands. The damage was done by the sharp aluminum fins that spring outward as the rocket leaves the launching tube: his right hand had been completely severed and lay in the dirt near his feet; his left hand hung from his arm by mere shreds of bone and flesh. He was rushed to a nearby aid station, where the bleeding was slowed, and he was then flown immediately to Phu Bai, where the surgeons were able to save his remaining hand.

As Bob told us the story, I couldn't help but notice how high his spirits were. He explained that he didn't mind losing a hand as long as he didn't have to go back to Eight-Klick Ville. He also expressed concern for the lieutenant who had caused the tragedy. Bob had found out that he had lost two fingers from the back blast of the rocket. He wanted to see the lieutenant, so he could ease his mind about the horrible accident.

After three days of rest and healing, the small, tattered group of Alpha Company's casualties was separated and sent in different directions. Some went to the 8th Field Hospital in Nha Trang; the rest, including myself, went to a huge medical complex in Cam Ranh Bay called the 9th Convalescent Center. The sprawling hospital grounds were nestled among the sloping hills that rolled gradually into the emerald green waters of the bay. The bay was beautiful, with wide sandy beaches and crystal-clear water, but was full of sharks cruising up and down like enemy submarines. We were made to swim in the salty waters to speed the healing process. It was not uncommon to be beckoned from the surf by a guard waving a red flag and frantically blowing a whistle. His job was watching for sharks. If one was spotted, a Huey was called in from a nearby air base. The chopper would hover over the shark and the two gunners would blaze away at their prey as it writhed in the surf and turned the green water red.

After two days at Cam Ranh, I was again taken to the operating facilities, where my thumb was reopened so the broken bone could be set. I expressed concern about not being able to use my thumb again, but I guess I was really hoping that's what the diagnosis would be; without full use of my left hand perhaps I wouldn't be sent back into combat. Since wounds healed fast in the saltwater of Cam Ranh Bay, my stay would be limited to two-and-a-half weeks. The abundance of rest and good food had begun to make me realize how much I missed home. The hours resting and thinking began to fray my nerves: the stark reality that I would soon be returning to the boonies haunted me.

When I was checked and released by the doctors, I was sent to the 101st Replacement Center at Bien Hoa to catch a military hop back to the Hue-Phu Bai airport. It took nearly a day and a half of flying on several C-130s to reach my destination. All I owned were the clothes on my back and a rifle that had been issued with a bandolier of ammo in Bien Hoa. Upon landing in Phu Bai, it was now up to me to hitchhike the twenty some miles back to LZ Sally. I set out walking the streets of Hue. Before I had gone a half mile, I was approached by a young Vietnamese boy wearing a wide grin and a Superman T-shirt. Noticing the insignia on my jungle hat, he shouted, *"Tung tse! Tung tse!* You want numba one boom boom?"* (Translation: "Sergeant! Sergeant! You want a first-class girl?") I motioned him away with a wave of my hand, but he grabbed my shirt and began to pull me back toward a small row of hootches. "Didi! Didi!" I shouted as I pulled away and drew my hand back in a gesture of slapping him. He again reached for me and beckoned, "Numba one boom boom. I take you my sista. Okay?" I swung my hand as though I was trying to knock his head off, but deliberately missed him. He jumped back and proceeded to curse me so fluently I could have sworn he was a GI.

It wasn't long before I flagged down a Marine driving a flatbed tractor-trailer loaded with large crates headed for the DMZ. He was a tall, skinny private with wiry muscles that bulged through the black, sweaty skin on his bare arms as he fought the steering wheel of the bouncing, lurching truck. It took us only minutes to discover we had grown up less than fifty miles apart back in North Carolina. By the time he stopped the truck and left me near the gate of LZ Sally, we had become good friends.

Arriving back at Alpha's supply hootch, I was glad to see some of my friends and catch up on the news from the past three-and-a-half weeks. First, I was given a whole mailbag full of "goodie" packages. I gave half of them to the supply personnel and administration clerks, saving the rest to take out to the field and divide among my buddies. Our company clerk, Andy Anderson, then filled me in on some of the horrible events that had happened while I was in the hospital. The last remaining platoon leader who had come over with us from Fort Campbell had been killed: 2nd Lt. Gary Hampton had been walking beside a tank on the edge of Eight Klick when the track of the rumbling monster detonated a large land mine. The blast caught Lieutenant Hampton in the midsection and nearly tore him in half.

There was also a sickening story from Cocoa Beach. Charlie Company was pulling security at Cocoa when a chopper load of new replacements was flown out to join them. Charlie Company had a couple of buck sergeants who were total idiots and took pride in playing jokes on cherries. The two would take a grenade, unscrew the handle and remove the blasting cap, screw the handle back on the grenade, then pull the pin and toss it to some green replacement. As the cherries scrambled for cover, they would double over with laughter as the dud grenade lay harmlessly on the ground. The horrible accident occurred when these two foolish E-5s were manning bunkers on the southern perimeter. They walked up to a new replacement and introduced themselves. As several soldiers watched from bunkers nearby, one of the sergeants pulled a grenade from his pocket, nonchalantly pulled the pin, and stuck the grenade in the cherry's face. The private instantly turned and ran for cover. As the jokesters stood there laughing, the grenade exploded, killing both of them instantly. Waste and foolishness such as this occurred frequently—unfortunately, there were many idiots who wore a uniform and called themselves soldiers. The investigation of the incident concluded that one of the buck sergeants had obviously picked up a live grenade, thinking it was the rigged, harmless one.

Returning to the field, I was introduced to our new platoon sergeant, who had already been tagged with the nickname "Super Leg." He was an aging Korean War veteran who looked as though he should be laid up in some VA hospital instead of humping the jungles and rice paddies of Vietnam. The Army had scraped the bottom of the barrel to come up with this antique NCO. He was arrogant and obnoxious, constantly reminding us of how bad he had it in the Korean War. He had never jumped from an airplane—the reason for his being dubbed "Super Leg."

He and I got off to a bad start when I questioned his reason for taking Tony Briley from my squad and making him his RTO. I never would have said anything to another outranking NCO, but I noticed that "ol' 3-5" (his radio call sign) had somehow talked Tony into carrying all of his heavy gear so that all he had in his rucksack was a rolled-up poncho liner and a change of socks. He didn't get along well with any of the squad leaders, and for some reason he picked out me as his scapegoat. He took advantage of every opportunity to assign me and my squad as many dirty details as possible.

One confrontation between us occurred over our ration of beer and soda. Two cans of soft drink and two cans of beer for each member of the company were flown out each week to be distributed. My squad was out on patrol that day, and by the time we returned to the company, the canned drinks, supplies, and C rations had been handed out. We collected our C rats and supplies, and never thought about the drinks since we had no idea they had arrived.

A couple of days later, Tony Briley told me that our squad's beer and soda had been stuffed neatly in Super Leg's rucksack since we had not been around to claim them. Now our sergeant would sit by himself at night and drink three or four of them at a time.

I was furious and immediately went to confront him about the matter. He had just walked down to a nearby stream to shave, leaving his rucksack beside Tony's pack and radio. When I picked up his pack, it was heavy with the full aluminum cans; he had instructed Tony to carry his poncho liner to make more room for his loot. I quickly opened up his ruck, had Tony stack the cans in my arms, and took the drinks back to the squad members. I popped the tops on all of the drinks and instructed them to drink them up or pour them out.

When ol' 3-5 realized what had happened, he stormed over to me all red-faced and puffing steam like an old locomotive. I stood quietly and waited to see what he was going to say. After listening to his threats and profanities, I told him that if he wanted to take up the matter with the CO, I would be happy to oblige. Realizing he had no case against me, he tightened his jaw and cursed all the way back to his shade tree.

After that incident, Super Leg began to put pressure on Van Long, knowing Bud and I thought a lot of him. He would pick on him unmercifully. Once he even called him a "gook" to his face, which made Van Long angry as hell—he shouted back that ol' 3-5 and Ho Chi Minh were "numba ten."

Within the same week of my return, a platoon of ARVNs was sent out to work with us. They were the most ragtag group of South Vietnamese soldiers we had been involved with. All they seemed interested in was seeing how many cans of C rations they could collect in a sandbag. When making sweeps through the VC-infested hamlets of Eight Klick, they were always found at the rear of the column where it was safer from booby traps and snipers. When we did force the ARVNs to walk up front with us, they were extremely nervous over the slightest movement. One night, while moving through a sector of Eight Klick under the illumination of a circling flare ship, a young Vietnamese soldier, working with our platoon, shouted "VC! VC!" and cranked up his outdated BAR (Browning automatic rifle) at a nearby hootch. A blood-curdling scream came from near the hootch as two large hogs came charging through our ranks, leaving a third porcine companion dead in the bushes.

As we moved on through the village that night, Lieutenant Melton asked if anyone had seen our platoon sergeant—he was unable to raise him on the radio. We had been so intent on our movement through the hamlets that no one had even noticed him missing. Joey Miller took his squad back to find him and returned with the news that ol' 3-5 was huddled in a bomb crater with one of our machine-gun teams completely surrounding him. It was obvious he had gotten cold feet. (One of the machine-gunners later informed us that they had been ordered to stay back and provide rear security.) A short time later they caught up with us, and we continued on through the village. Our movement was halted intermittently because of a lone VC sniper taking shots at us with an RPG rocket launcher. Our nerves were taut, and we were easily spooked by anything that moved.

As we made our way around a gradually sloping sector of the village, someone excitedly brought our attention to enemy troop movement in the wide rice paddy below us. At a distance of at least 200 yards appeared the ghostly figures of a platoon-sized element of VC. The pale light of the flares above us clearly revealed dark shadows making their way from the village toward a large wooded area. Lieutenant Melton quickly formed us up on line behind a long berm, and we prepared to fire simultaneously on the enemy soldiers. This was the opportunity we had been looking for: to get even with the Viet Cong. It seemed too perfect to be true, however, and someone asked if they might possibly be friendly troops. Lieutenant Melton sensed this also, as we all did, so he held his command to fire and called the CO about the possibility of friendlies being in the area. A short time passed as we waited on word from battalion and watched the troops move slowly across our front. The message finally crackled back over the radio receiver: the nearest American or South Vietnamese troops were more than two miles away. Lieutenant Melton passed along the word to prepare to fire. Adrenaline rushed through our veins as the whole platoon of M16 rifles, M79 grenade launchers, and M60 machine guns trained toward the enemy troops, waiting for the order, "Fire!"

Seconds seemed like hours; finally the command reached our ears and was quickly snuffed out by the din of discharging weapons. Flame-red tracers raced each other to the target area and then flew skyward as they ricocheted off the dry rice paddy. Yellow and white explosions from the grenade launchers danced on and off like the flashing lights of the PX pinball machines back at Fort Campbell. As we reloaded weapons during a slight lull in the firing, several GIs screamed a war whoop, like charging Indians in the old Western movies. There was no doubt we were dealing out death, for we could see enemy soldiers falling like flies trying to escape our blistering fire.

The enemy scattered, and silence fell as we ceased firing and waited to see what would happen next. I heard Lieutenant Melton acknowledge a transmission over his radio, and thought I detected a tone of fear and uncertainty in his voice. Quickly he passed down an order to cease all firing. As he continued to receive transmissions from Captain Keever, he cursed loudly into the receiver. A hush fell over us as we realized something was very wrong. Had we just fired on American troops? With a shaky voice, our lieutenant confirmed our fears: the VC soldiers were actually a lost element from the 502nd Infantry Battalion, which was working an AO adjacent to ours. A young, inexperienced platoon leader had gotten his men lost and they had strayed into our area of operation without notifying their headquarters of their dangerous situation. They had somehow managed to get out a radio message as we took them under fire. Their battalion headquarters had contacted ours, and the message was relayed to our company commander.

We were stunned at the possibility of having massacred a whole platoon of our comrades from a sister battalion. Luck was with us, however, or more so with them. Not a single trooper had been killed. Many of the GIs were wounded, though, and lay bleeding and suffering in the sharp stubble of the recently harvested rice paddy. We were instructed to stay away and let them care for their own casualties— headquarters feared the survivors might try to retaliate against us. We watched in agony and total silence as two dust-off choppers came in on the homing beacon of a strobe light and took on their load of bloody cargo. We were ordered to hold up for the rest of the night and set up a defensive perimeter. Battalion knew our morale had reached bottom, and we would have our minds on the tragic foul-up instead of our mission. It was on this night, as I sat alone in a foxhole and pondered the evening's horrible events, that a small seed of doubt germinated deep within my mind, and I began to have second thoughts about this madness called the Vietnam War.

Search-and-clear sweeps continued in Eight-Klick Ville for the next several days. Less than a week after our ambush on the GIs from the 502nd, we were extracted by Hueys to a small fire base called Mongoose. This newly constructed fire-support base lay at the northern end of Eight Klick and literally bristled with 105mm artillery pieces, providing support for the many elements of Screaming Eagles that humped the nearby boonies. We were to stay at Mongoose for a three-day rest period, providing bunker guard and filling sandbags. Our stay was costly, however, because Sp4 Jerry Walters was burned severely by a gasoline explosion, and Pfc Jim Wade nearly lost a finger from an exploding blasting cap. These types of noncombatant accidents constantly plagued the soldiers of Vietnam, regardless of their rank or MOS. We had grown callous to the pain and suffering of such injuries.

Our stay at Mongoose was cut short when intelligence reported a large element of North Vietnamese holed up in a small village near the coast. We packed our gear and drew fresh ammo. Moving beyond the razor-sharp coils of concertina wire, we waited on the sortie of Hueys that would deliver us to the enemy.

The 3rd Platoon went out on the second lift, following 1st Platoon. As the Hueys touched down, we jumped from the skids into a boiling, blinding sandstorm created by the powerful pitch of the rotor blades. The fine, white sand of the coastal flats filled our eyes, mouths, and nostrils and gave us the appearance of sugar-coated Christmas cookies. While the choppers flew back for the 2nd Platoon, we began to maneuver on the still-quiet village. As we worked our way over a brush-covered ridge, a lone enemy soldier announced his presence with an AK47, prematurely springing the ambush waiting for us. We stopped our forward movement and called in artillery to soften the enemy positions. We patiently waited while the enemy soldiers were blasted by the big guns. From our positions on the ridge, we had an advantage over the NVA and were able to spot them as they tried to escape the shelling. We easily picked them off with our machine guns and rifles.

When the shelling stopped, we moved into the village and searched for dead and wounded North Vietnamese. Approaching a nearby tree line, we were taken under fire by an enemy mortar team, sending us scrambling for cover in the trees to our front. Fortunately we found a long fighting trench, dug just inside the tree line, well hidden by the low-hanging boughs of several pine trees. The mortar rounds were landing dangerously close, so our FO, still observing from the ridge, called in supporting artillery to try to knock out the enemy mortar team. We crouched in the trench and watched the village again come under a brutal artillery attack. As the shells landed nearly a hundred yards away, one lone 155mm shell strayed and exploded in a small rice paddy to our immediate front. We instinctively crouched a little lower. In the next barrage, a shell landed a mere ten feet away from where we were hiding. The deafening explosion scared us nearly to death, and a large chunk of jagged shrapnel sliced a pine tree in two, dropping it across me and Jerald LeDeux. Fearing that the next shell would land on top of us, we grabbed for a smoke grenade to mark our positions and let Papa One, our forward observer, know exactly where one of his guns was incorrectly firing. He was one step ahead of us—having seen the shell crash into our platoon, he was already screaming over the radio for a cease-fire. We lay in the trench for several minutes until the wild firing of the artillery piece was corrected; then we resumed our push. A final surge through the village resulted in an enemy body count of seven with three prisoners taken. The element was not North Vietnamese, as we had thought, but mostly Viet Cong.

We stayed in the village that night without further signs of the enemy and shortly after dawn were told to prepare for another heliborne assault back to Eight-Klick Ville. This time there was a confirmed company of NVA. We waited on an emergency resupply of ammunition and C rations, and then took another half hour to choke down our breakfast and a cup of coffee. The day was still young when we found ourselves scrambling aboard Hueys that had squatted in a nearby paddy. The flight was short but refreshing as the cool morning air gushed through the open sides of the choppers and evaporated the cold sweat that glistened on our faces. Eight Klick appeared so peaceful in the morning mist, but we knew how treacherous it really was. Our choppers flew to the far end of Eight Klick, and banked sharply before flying over a remote hamlet, obviously our destination. We could see smoke and dust from artillery shells pummeling the enemy positions. We landed in an open rice paddy far from the tree line and immediately came under fire from RPG rockets and enemy mortars. Our only cover lay some fifty yards away in the form of a small canal. We must have given the enemy soldiers a good laugh as we raced for the banks of the canal and threw ourselves into the murky, leech-infested water. With only our heads visible above the canal banks, we quickly formed into platoons and decided on a method of approaching the distant village. The CO ordered our platoon to move out first. Without knowing where any of the enemy positions were, we formed up to race across the open, toward their waiting guns. As we climbed from the canal and crouched on its grassy edge, tragedy struck immediately. A new replacement, David Baker, was poised on the bank waiting on a signal to move toward the village when suddenly he lunged backward into the water. Someone grabbed him and pulled him from the canal. Blood gushed through his fingers as he clutched his face. The rest of us dropped back into the water as medics raced over to help the screaming GI. An NVA soldier had taken a well-aimed shot: the bullet had entered David's left eye, blown off the bridge of his nose, then made an exit out of his right eye.

It took four men to hold him down as the medics desperately tried to wrap his head and stop the bleeding. A dust-off was called in, and volunteers were asked to carry David further back out of mortar range. Mike Brinson jumped up to help his friend and before he could reach him, a bullet tore through his arm and blew splinters of bone out a large, gaping hole in the back of his elbow.

There was no doubt that we were up against crack troops; they had the advantage over us and were definitely making the most of it. The decision to remain in the canal was quickly agreed to, and the CO got on the horn and called in air strikes and heavy artillery. The big guns cranked up and covered the little village with another cloud of dust and smoke. While we watched the shells chew up the trees and hootches, a small FAC plane appeared and buzzed over the enemy positions. The NVA knew exactly what that small plane meant to them, and we could hear the chatter of their rifles as they tried to knock it from the sky. Less than five minutes after the FAC plane buzzed the village, two heavily armed navy Phantoms screamed over us and circled like falcons, waiting for a signal to swoop down toward their prey. The small, single-engine FAC plane maneuvered aerobatically over the burning village and marked target areas for the F4s with its smoke rockets. As soon as the Phantom pilots spotted the smoke from the phosphorous rockets, they peeled off in turn and screamed down toward their targets. Just before slamming into the earth they pulled out of the dive, dropped their bombs with pinpoint accuracy, then pitched their sleek aircraft into an ear-splitting ascent. It was appalling to witness the devastation they delivered—I felt a trace of pity for the enemy troops who had to withstand their attacks. When their bomb racks were empty, the jets made another run, dropping canisters of napalm on the dug-in enemy. As far away as we were, we could feel the intense heat from the billowing clouds of jellied gas that vomited from the ruptured pods. After the napalm, final runs were made with long bursts from their 20mm cannons. Before the two Phantoms had completed their mission, two more were on station, circling high above the village, waiting for their turn at the hidden enemy. Again we watched the sleek jets go through their maneuvers. The tiny village was totally destroyed by the brute power of the air strikes. It was beyond my imagination that anyone could have survived such a savage attack, but as soon as the second team of F4s completed its mission and flew back to a distant carrier, several enemy soldiers resumed their well-aimed shots at our heads as we peered over the banks of the canal. Luckily, no one was hit as the bullets splattered our faces with mud, but the aggressiveness of their defensive tactics forced us to spend the remainder of the day in the filthy waters of the canal.

More air strikes and artillery pounded the village as the hours went by. In the fading light of the day we searched for a dry perch on top of the canal dike so we could stretch out and get some much-needed sleep. Darkness found us clinging to a narrow dike like pigeons on a ledge. Half of us pulled guard; the other half slept. I chose not to lie down on the muddy dike but instead tried to sleep sitting up with my head between my knees and my arms wrapped around my shins. The tension and fatigue from the long day forced me into a deep sleep, allowing the law of gravity to sneak up on me. As I slumbered with my buttocks and feet stuck tightly in the black mud, I leaned a little too far to one side and was abruptly awakened by the cool waters of the canal surging over my body. Waking up underwater will totally disorient anyone, and I must have floundered around in the muddy canal for at least a minute before climbing back to my small perch. The darkness concealed my identity, but still there was uncontrollable laughter from nearby buddies. When morning came they were asking who had fallen off the dike during the night. There was no doubt, since I was pasted from head to foot with chocolate-colored slime.

After a quick meal of C's, we started our move toward the village where only the day before an invisible enemy had held us at bay. As we approached the smoldering village, we drew no fire. The North Vietnamese soldiers who had not fallen victim to the savage bombardment had escaped during the night. The village was in ruins—we found bodies lying everywhere as we picked our way through the wreckage, collecting strewn, abandoned weapons.

Later that day four large tanks joined our company with orders to help us sweep through one end of Eight Klick and push enemy resistance toward a blocking force made up of ARVNs and elements from the 502nd Infantry. Our push through the hamlets was uneventful. We settled in for the night, positioning the tanks around our defensive perimeter. As we were digging in, Lieutenant Melton informed me that I would take an LP to a nearby tree line. I picked two of the most dependable men in the squad and moved out in the dark for a small graveyard nestled near the distant village. We finally located the cluster of graves and chose one bordered by a low concrete wall. We had taken great pains to move to the graveyard undetected, and it seemed as though we would spend a quiet night at our listening post. However, the respected Mr. Charles Cong had seen us.

We were still awake, sitting quietly in the dark, when the "whump" of a large mortar tube sent us sprawling behind the concrete wall of the grave mound. I was sure the projectile was meant for the company perimeter, but it had landed just a few yards to our rear. A second round landed even closer, convincing us that we were the target of the deadly missiles. I grabbed the radio mike and called for our forward observer. Papa One was on the horn immediately and asked for a grid in order to call for artillery support. Not yet knowing the location of the mortar tube, I rose to my knees and searched the tree line for the flash of the gun. Two more rounds were fired. Spotting the yellow tube flash, I drew a grid on the gun position. As I called the grid coordinate to Papa One, a projectile landed to our immediate left, spraying our concrete foxhole with hot shrapnel. I knew at once that I had been hit, for a searing pain shot through my shoulder and ran up my neck. We lay in the dark and waited for our artillery rounds to quiet the enemy mortar tube. When the arty shells began slamming into the trees, I again climbed to my knees to call an adjustment on the firing. The shrapnel wound in my shoulder was not serious enough to abort our listening post, but by morning my shoulder was still bleeding and had become stiff and very painful. Returning to the company perimeter, Doc Smith checked my shoulder and tagged me for extraction back to LZ Sally. The wound was not bad enough to be taken to the 22nd Surg, but it would need treatment in order to prevent infection.

I flew back to Sally on the afternoon log ship and sought medical attention for the small shrapnel wound. After a couple of doctors looked at my shoulder, they determined that the shrapnel was too deep to remove without surgery, so the wound was bandaged and left alone to heal over the deeply embedded piece of metal. I stayed at LZ Sally and simply took it easy while carrying my arm around in a sling. One afternoon I was shuffling along one of the oil-covered roads on my way back from the PX tent. My right hand was full of cigarettes and toilet articles that I had purchased for myself and my buddies, and my left arm was in a sling, so I was unable to salute a young second lieutenant who approached me on the dusty road. I nodded to him and said, "Hello, sir," only to have him halt me and proceed to bless me out for not saluting an officer. His untanned face and new jungle fatigues and boots made it obvious that he had just arrived from the States. "How long have you been in country, sir?" I asked. This made him madder than a hornet, and he barked out orders for me to stand at attention and salute. Realizing my predicament was getting embarrassingly out of hand, I informed him that those of us who had come over from Fort Campbell had been instructed not to salute anyone below a major and that those orders had come down from brigade headquarters. Those specific instructions were given in order to keep from having to salute officers in the field and possibly identifying them to the enemy soldiers. In order to simplify the directive, we were informed that the order also applied to base camps, so captains and lieutenants should not expect their troops to salute. The second lieutenant quickly calmed down and began groping for words to conceal his embarrassment. Just to get back at him in a subtle way, I turned to walk away and commented, "That's okay, sir. When you've been in country a little while longer you'll find out about all those things."

After almost a week of excellent medical attention, my shoulder stopped draining and healed over. I had enjoyed my brief stay at base camp during which I could shower daily, eat hot meals, sleep on a cot, and spend the evenings playing poker instead of sitting in a foxhole. I was preparing my gear to return to the company when First Sergeant Soward asked me to be responsible for getting ten new cherries ready to go to the boonies. They had been members of Alpha Company for two days and were almost ready to be sent to the fields. They seemed like a good bunch except for one private first class who spent most of his time trying to show everyone just how tough he was. Most of us chose to ignore him, but his personality convinced me that I did not want him assigned to my squad. It took both flights of the afternoon log and de-log to get all of us out to the boonies. My mistake of flying out on the second load allowed the new "tough boy" to be assigned to the 3rd Platoon. He had flown out on the first lift and was put in another squad, quickly earning the nickname "Motormouth."

The very next day we were sweeping through Eight Klick and came upon several decomposing NVA bodies that one of our sister companies had left a few days earlier. All of us chose to stay as far away as possible from the stench of the bodies except for "Motormouth," who cockily walked over to one of the corpses and kicked it in the head. To his surprise, the skull split open and covered his boot and pant leg with slime and maggots, accompanied by the most horrible smell imaginable.

Those of us who witnessed his foolish act broke into laughter as he raced behind a hootch and uncontrollably threw up.

Later in the day we were ordered to move into a thickly wooded area and lay low while waiting on orders for a critical night search in a nearby village. Army intelligence had informed us that the Viet Cong were holding a tax-collection meeting within the small hamlet. Our mission would be to surround them and capture as many as possible. We were to wait on darkness and move in quickly while Bravo Company set up a cordon on the far side of the village. Our only problem was a wide, shallow river we would have to wade across in order to sneak into the rear of the hamlet—there was the possibility of stepping in deep holes and being held underwater by the weight of our heavy gear. The only other approach to the hamlet was across open rice fields. We chose the former.

The black of night allowed us to move quickly toward our destination. Reaching the river, we split up into platoons in order to cross in three separate columns. A full moon hung white in the night sky and clearly outlined us against the shimmering water as we waded in up to our chests. It was inevitable that we would be detected under such dangerous conditions. We all kept our eyes on a small sampan floating downstream from us with a lantern hanging from its bow. As the head of our columns climbed out on the far bank of the river, three shots rang out as a signal of danger. The boat lantern was quickly extinguished and the small craft glided away in the shadows. The boat had served as a sentry and had played its part well as an early-warning system to the VC within the village. Our plan of surprise had been spoiled, but our orders were to push on and try to drive the enemy toward Bravo Company, lying in the dark hoping to catch the evasive Cong.

Knowing our foe had been warned, we were extremely nervous about the ghostly silence that hung over the village. The hamlet was shaped like a horseshoe with a large rice paddy in its center. For some strange reason, we were ordered to move to the center of the paddy where there was no cover. We stood out clearly against the yellow rice stubble as the moon continued to dodge among the scattered clouds. Suddenly, a long burst from a machine gun sent us scrambling for the nearby cover of the two-foot-high dikes. Some of our troops, closer to the tree line, fired back with short bursts of rifles and machine guns as we lay in the open and waited for the feared "whump" of enemy mortar tubes. The distant drone of a chopper engine circled high above our heads. Lieutenant Melton passed the word that it was White Falcon, our battalion commander. Having blown our mission, our next objective would be to either charge into the village or withdraw from the precarious position in which we had placed ourselves. Minutes dragged by as we lay behind the rice dikes and waited on orders for our next move. There was commotion within the company headquarters group nearby, then First Sergeant Soward stood and turned on a strobe light. We couldn't believe our eyes. Everyone cursed—this ridiculous act would definitely bring enemy fire upon us. None of us knew what was going on, but we found out later that White Falcon had ordered our CO to briefly turn on a strobe light so his chopper pilot could locate our position. His chopper was obviously disoriented in the dark, and he wanted to make sure of our location before instructing Captain Keever on our next move.

By now, there was no doubt that the Viet Cong had dispersed and could no longer be found within the village. However, orders came down for us to push on and clear it of any VC suspects. Movement through the village was slow and treacherous as we feared the deadly booby traps that only the enemy knew how to avoid. In less than two hours, we had swept the entire village and linked up with Bravo Company. We considered ourselves lucky, for our only casualty was one soldier who had suffered a slight leg wound from a punji stake. Unsuccessful operations like this one were common because the cunning Viet Cong soldiers controlled the night. They were smart and highly evasive, especially when dealing with a large infantry company that had trouble moving swiftly and undetected.

Several days passed, lengthening our stay in the treacherous Eight-Klick Ville. A scout dog and handler had joined us, along with a new squad of National Police (South Vietnamese), who were easily recognized by their brown camouflage fatigues. The scout dog was a large, beautiful German shepherd, who was meaner than a snake. He seemed to take pleasure in lunging at us if we ventured too close. He tore a large chunk from the seat of Roger Clapeckni's pants before his handler could pull him off. Roger jokingly talked about spiking his dog food with a hand grenade. The scout dogs came in handy though, because many of them could sniff booby traps. This particular dog helped us herd civilians as we cleared the villages in search of VC suspects. One night in particular, we were sweeping a populated village and moving the civilians to a gathering point where they would be interrogated and held for further questioning or released. There must have been fifty to a hundred civilians of all ages in our cortege, and they were causing us problems by moving slowly and not staying bunched together. This was not only dangerous to us, but to them, for it increased the chances of triggering booby traps and being cut off from the GIs working in front of us. After hassling with the civilians for at least an hour, someone suggested that we let the scout dog ride herd on them like a flock of sheep. The handler and his dog were called over, and it took them less than a minute to round up the frightened Vietnamese and get them moving smartly down the trails. The dog strained at his leash and snapped at the heels of the scurrying natives. We let him enjoy himself, since it took the pressure off us and allowed our noisy group to keep up with the lead element. I did feel sorry for the children, for they were extremely frightened by the dog, and several of us moved among them trying to calm them down. The civilians were led crying and jabbering into the center of a large graveyard, where they spent the night with us and were interrogated the next morning. Only two or three male suspects were detained for further questioning; the rest of the frightened group were released and allowed to return to their hamlets.

Working with the civilians was a sensitive and tedious chore, since our objective was to help them, yet still maintain control in order to prevent dangerous situations from occurring between them and us. The majority of our troops were sympathetic to the South Vietnamese, especially the children, but there was always the possibility that one of them would toss a grenade at us, or play upon our sympathy during the day, then track us during the night. Sometimes the frustrations inherent in the situation led to shameful behavior, even atrocities.

Once, in Eight-Klick Ville, we were searching a small cluster of hootches divided by a deep canal; our platoon was on one side and the 2nd Platoon was on the other, allowing us a front-row seat to a horrible incident we could not prevent. An E-5 sergeant from 2nd Platoon, a man with a reputation as a tough guy, came across a dilapidated hootch that was shelter for an old woman and a mentally retarded man. Receiving no cooperation from the Vietnamese man, the sergeant pulled him from the hootch and shouted loudly at him, "VC! VC!" Not knowing his intentions, we watched from across the canal as the buck sergeant dragged his prisoner down a trail that paralleled the water's edge. The old woman wailed and pleaded for her loved one, but none of us interfered—past experiences had taught us all to stay out of another

GI's business when he was venting his anger and frustrations. Interfering usually led to bitter quarreling and sometimes fighting among ourselves. As we watched the unnecessary brutalizing of the pitifully frightened Vietnamese, we had no idea what the end result would be. We figured the civilian would soon be released to join the old lady.

Before any of us could react, the E-5 squad leader shoved the stumbling man into a trail bunker and fired his rifle on automatic into the bunker entrance. I grew sick at the thought of the cold-blooded murder we had just witnessed, and several of us cursed loudly across the canal at the young sergeant. I felt like shooting him as he laughed at the old woman, who had thrown herself across the opening of the small bunker, wailing and screaming over the loss of her son. Incidents like this were rare, but did happen when soldiers reached the breaking point.

Days went by and we wondered if we would ever be pulled out of Eight-Klick Ville and assigned to another area of operation. Many of us were getting trigger-happy and paranoid from working under the constant strain; we were becoming careless and were firing up everything that wasn't wearing army fatigues. Late one night we moved toward a small village in which a squad of VC was thought to be hiding. Our platoon was responsible for approaching the village from the west; we were having to cover a long distance in a short period of time in order to rendezvous with another platoon. As we moved through the paddies and wooded areas, we periodically sent out scouts on patrol to clear a danger zone before committing our entire platoon. John Boyd and Ernie Parton were now forward, searching a small group of hootches. Minutes dragged by as we waited on their return. Suddenly, a machine gun cranked up at the rear of our column. The gun continued firing for several seconds, then stopped as abruptly as it had started. No one moved a muscle as we searched the darkness for signs of trouble. Then a mournful cry for help broke the silence. It was John Boyd's voice, but it was mysteriously coming from our rear, where the machine gun had been firing. It didn't take long to figure out what had happened. John and Ernie had become disoriented in the dark and had walked past our column on their return, wandering around before stumbling across our rear security position. Fast Herm Hope had spotted them in the distance and, thinking they were VC, emptied a belt of M60 ammo into the shadowy figures. John had been shot in the foot and Ernie had taken two slugs through the chest. Our mission was delayed as a medevac was called in. Fast Herm was tagged and sent in also—the enormity of his mistake had sent him into shock.

After evacuating our casualties, we hurried on to our destination and searched for the Viet Cong, who were nowhere to be found. We then moved into a deserted village and set up an ambush along a winding canal. The rest of the night was peaceful, allowing us to get some rest, but morning brought another tragedy to our weary platoon.

As dawn's first light painted the sky a pale gray, we began to stir, stretching the kinks from our tired muscles. Having moved into our ambush during the middle of the night, we had simply picked out a place in the dark and stretched out on the hard ground. Our three-man positions were grouped in a tight perimeter, with four positions situated along the canal and Lieutenant Melton's CP stationed in the middle. I had just been awakened by our last guard when the distinct crack of an AK47 sent us all scrambling for cover in the wet grass and weeds. A long automatic burst of twenty or thirty rounds chattered just across the canal from us, sending ricocheting bullets zipping through the grass and snipping small branches from the brush. The firing ceased in a matter of seconds, and was quickly followed by our rifles and machine guns retaliating against the invisible enemy. A mad minute of firing was directed against the thick brush and trees on the opposite bank of the canal, but no one knew what he was shooting at.

When the din of the weapons ceased, there was a desperate scream for a medic. I turned around to see Lieutenant Melton charging through the brush toward the canal in an effort to assist his wounded soldiers. His RTO called over the radio for a dust-off. Before long, members of Joey Miller's squad carried out a body wrapped in a poncho. As they struggled to haul it through the brush, I noticed a blood-covered hand protruding from a tear in the poncho. Someone mentioned Wayne Timmons's name as the one who had been killed. Three others had been severely wounded and were quickly brought away from the canal and carried to a clearing in order to be choppered off to Phu Bai.

When our wounded had been taken care of, we fell back and called in artillery from fire base Mongoose. The VC were long gone, but Lieutenant Melton felt as we did. We simply wanted to blow apart the area as a statement of our anger and frustration. We were less than a mile from Mongoose, meaning that the 105mm shells would have to be lobbed into the target area. We lay low as the explosions shattered the calm of morning, and we were amazed that we could see the shells against the gray sky, slowly arching over our heads and falling less than 200 yards to our front.

Harassment from the VC, fatigue from lack of sleep, and fear of becoming a casualty were turning most of us into animals. We were losing our patience with the civilians and were starting to treat them as though they were to blame for our low morale and constant state of weariness. Shortly after Wayne Timmons was killed, an incident occurred that proved how we were all being affected. We were crossing a vast stretch of rice fields when someone noticed a young man running away from us toward a distant tree line. We shouted, *"Dung Lai! Dung Lai!"* for him to stop, but he kept running in spite of our warnings. I dropped my rucksack and helmet and started chasing him. I was gaining on him, when a single shot flew by me and sent the young Vietnamese sprawling in the dry rice paddy. I turned to see who had fired and was shocked to find it was Captain Keever. I knelt down to roll over the Vietnamese and realized he was only fourteen or fifteen years old. Speaking to him in French, I was surprised when he answered me in fluent French, "Please don't kill! Don't kill!" As the medics dressed the boy's wound, I noticed that our CO seemed ashamed of what he had done. We learned that the young boy had been told by the VC that the Americans killed innocent civilians just for fun; now, because of this shameful act by our commanding officer, he had been convinced this was true.

A squad of Vietnamese National Police had been working with us for several days, and although they had proven themselves to be highly effective as we dealt with the enemy during the day, their efficiency rating greatly decreased at night. Added to this was the language problem—they spoke only a few words of English.

On this particular night our entire company was to move across the width of Eight Klick and surround a small hamlet for an early-morning sweep. The group of NPs had been assigned to my squad, and we were to bring up rear security, since no one wanted the NPs near the lead element. As we moved across the darkened village, a narrow footbridge slowed our entire column, since only one soldier could cross at a time. That was where my squad got into trouble. Our advancement was held up to allow the lead platoon to search out a danger zone, and one of the Vietnamese soldiers attached to us was halted by a GI just as he was about to cross the rickety footbridge. He sat down on the bank and waited, and then did not understand the GI's signal to "pick up and move out." The NP continued to sit in the dark while the rest of the company moved on without us. I was at the very end of the column, and at least ten minutes passed before I became suspicious and moved forward to the bridge to see what was wrong. I found the NP still sitting patiently, waiting on a signal he obviously had missed some ten minutes earlier. When I realized our predicament, I nearly panicked.

There I was right in the middle of Eight Klick with two other GIs and four South Vietnamese who spoke very little English. Luckily I had a radioman with me. I collected myself and called for assistance. First Sergeant Soward got on the horn and proceeded to instruct me through the pitch-black trails so we could catch up with the remainder of the company. I rounded up our small group, trying to calm the two GIs who were cursing the young Vietnamese. We quietly moved across the footbridge and gathered on the opposite bank. I took the lead along with the radioman and put the NPs in the middle with the third GI behind them. Moving a few feet down the dark trails seemed like several miles, and I felt as though my heart would jump into my throat. The calm, steady voice of First Sergeant Soward was leading us through turn after turn when suddenly a burst of automatic-rifle fire sent scarlet tracers zipping past us in the night. I lay still, with my face flat against the dirt, then slowly turned and crawled like a reptile to check on the others. Pressing the radio receiver against my ear, I could hear the first sergeant calling, "Alpha Three X-ray! Alpha Three X-ray! Come in! Are you all right? Over." My voice shaking with fear, I answered, "This is Three X-ray. All's okay! Just keep talking and let me know where you are so we can get out of here! Over."

We waited several minutes, then picked ourselves up to try it again. After at least fifteen minutes of stumbling and groping along the trails, I suddenly met face-to-face with a lone figure standing quietly in the dark. I was just about to pull the trigger when I heard, "Is that you, Sarge?" Recognizing "Top" Soward's voice, I almost shouted out loud. I took a moment to brief him on what had happened. I was touched greatly that he had come back into the village by himself to locate us and reunite us with the rest of the company. Before we found our way out of the village, another burst of machine-gun fire broke the silence; our point platoon killed two unsuspecting VC who had wandered into their midst.

The next day we continued our search-and-clear operations through the hamlets while Bud Dykes took a small patrol to clear a cluster of hootches on the far side of a large rice paddy. They had been gone nearly two hours when rifle fire rang out in the distance and brought our attention to the safety of Bud's patrol. A radio message soon followed, informing us that the small element had caught three Viet Cong crossing a wide canal and had shot them before they reached the far side. Due to the strong current, their bodies had not been retrieved, but their weapons had been found and would be brought back to the company.

When Bud brought in the patrol, he turned over the mud-covered rifles and briefed our CO about the three enemy bodies. Captain Keever and Lieutenant Melton were pleased, and it was reported that Alpha Company had chalked up three more on their body-count list. Bud soon lumbered over to me, grinning slyly, and quietly confided the real story. His patrol had been approached by a small boy who led them to the canal and pointed to a shallow place in the water where he had seen some VC throw their weapons. The rifles were pulled from the slimy bottom and collected for sending back to LZ Sally. Bud's patrol had then fired their rifles into the canal and claimed they had been shooting at fleeing VC. They had made up the story in order to give our company another chance at sending in a body count to battalion headquarters. We were constantly under pressure to turn in a body count, and the word was out that companies with the greatest number would get to spend more time at Cocoa Beach. It was an accepted thing to cheat on a body count report—all of us had been guilty of this.

It was sheer coincidence that in less than two days we learned we were scheduled to return to Cocoa Beach. Soon we would be able to swim in the warm waters of the Gulf of Tonkin and stuff ourselves with the delicious navy chow. This four-day R & R, however, would not turn out as we expected: our well-deserved rest was destined to be interrupted by a monstrous typhoon sweeping in from the South China Sea.

We had been at Cocoa Beach for less than twelve hours when the skies darkened and the surf began to boil and foam and slam against the giant sand dunes that kept the ocean away from the small navy base. On our second day the savage storm moved in for the kill, but a slight change in its course steered the center of the typhoon north toward the DMZ, saving us from the maximum force of the torrential wind and rain. The small navy base staggered under the force of the giant waves and howling wind; our major concern turned from providing security for the fuel depot to simply surviving the onslaught of the rising tide and the deadly roofing tin and lumber that sailed about, flattening everyone and everything in its path. Most of the hootches lost their roofs, and it was impossible to escape the driving rain—we were cold and wet during the day and night, no matter where we tried to hide. Three to four feet of ocean water covered the camp, and the hootches that still had roofs were flooded with dirty water that smelled of human waste washed up from the latrine sumps. I took refuge in a large administrative building and sat up all night listening to radio messages from a naval vessel that was having trouble riding out the storm.

Two days later the typhoon had played itself out and the warm sun returned to help calm down the angry ocean. We crawled out from whatever shelter we had found, gawking at the wreckage and devastation that surrounded us. The naval camp had been nearly destroyed by an enemy force more powerful than anything the North Vietnamese or Viet Cong could have thrown at it. The remainder of our stay was spent helping the navy personnel pick up the pieces of the shattered camp. Sling loads of tin and lumber were flown in under the bellies of twin-rotored Chinooks, and it wasn't long before we had the small camp back on its feet.

While still at Cocoa, Bud approached me, saying that Van Long had something very important he wanted to talk to us about. I had no earthly idea what Van had on his mind, and my inquiries only made Bud laugh, shake his head, and answer, "Just wait! You'll find out." I noticed an air of nervousness and uncertainty in Van Long that I had never known him to possess. Bud stood by and said nothing, while Van Long jabbered in broken English about his family who lived in Quang Dien. I could make out from his story that he wanted them to live closer to Phu Bai, where he could see them more often; but still not understanding the meaning of his mixed-up tale, I turned to Bud with a puzzled look on my face and asked what was going on.

The answer was simple: Van wanted us to buy him a house in Phu Bai. He knew he could count on Bud and me before anyone else, yet he was nervous about asking us for the two hundred dollars he needed to purchase the modest cinderblock home. His main concern in relocating his family was to get his small children away from busy Highway One where military trucks rumbled over the potholes just feet away from where his children played. Between the two of us, Bud and I were able to scrape together just a little more than two hundred dollars—I had sixty dollars (in MPC) on me and Bud came up with the balance. Van Long stood with his mouth open and stared at the military money as we counted it out.

Van's face beamed when Bud handed him the wad of bills, and it pleased us too to know we had just gained a lifelong friend in the poor but proud Vietnamese soldier. Van Long, like most South Vietnamese, thought all Americans were filthy rich. Bud and I had emptied our pockets to buy him a new home, and we laughed about how he must figure all we had to do was look in another pocket and there would be more money to spend.

As we were preparing our gear to leave Cocoa Beach, First Sergeant Soward told me he wanted me to leave the 3rd Platoon and work with the headquarters group. His demanding schedule required that he spend more time at LZ Sally, and he wanted me to remain in the fields and handle the log ships and supplies that were sent to us daily. I had strong feelings about leaving my squad, but the thought of not having to pull ambush or LP patrols was enough to sway me. I would still be with the company but would have the responsibility of keeping it supplied and fed, instead of working with a squad of riflemen and grenadiers. C rations, hot food, fresh water, medical supplies, fatigues, boots, equipment, and ammunition were needed daily for the functioning of more than a hundred infantrymen. Now I would be the one they would point a finger at if any of these needs went unmet.

I decided to take the responsibility and move over to the headquarters element. Leaving my squad wasn't quite as hard as I had imagined, since most of the old-time vets had been either killed or sent back to the States because of serious wounds. Bud took over the position of squad leader, and one week later was promoted to staff sergeant (E-6). He well deserved the promotion, for he was one of the best soldiers Alpha Company had ever seen. He never said a word about my decision to leave the platoon. We had become as close as brothers over the past several months, and our friendship helped us to understand each other's feelings.

Three Chinooks flew in and picked us up on the storm-littered beaches; they then lumbered off to drop our entire company onto the rice paddies surrounding Eight Klick. It appeared as though we were permanently assigned to this dreaded place, and many of us would have gladly returned to the dangerous mountains if given the chance. I stayed busy with my new responsibilities and within days had made several new friends within the headquarters group. I became especially close to our senior medic, who was a declared conscientious objector. His religious beliefs prohibited him from carrying a weapon, but his personal beliefs had led him to enlist in the Army and serve in the Vietnam War. "Doc" Brailey was a gentle-natured fellow from Wisconsin who had a tender spot in his heart for the children of Vietnam; he spent his free time playing with them and giving medical attention to the needy. Since Doc didn't carry a weapon, we made a pact that I would take care of him with my rifle, and he would take care of me if I were wounded.

Days passed without Alpha Company participating in any major operations. VC activity in Eight Klick was subsiding because of constant pressure from our battalion and one from the 502nd Infantry. We heard rumors that a major operation was in the making, but we would have to spend several more days trying to avoid the booby traps and snipers of Eight-Klick Ville before we would engage the enemy in the Battle of Vinh Loc.

It was during the middle of the night that our CO received word from battalion headquarters that we would participate in a massive heliborne assault during sunup the next morning. Word was given to the platoon leaders to have their troops ready to move at least two hours before dawn. We figured this was probably the "big one" that we had heard about. As first light crawled over the horizon, sorties of Hueys and Chinooks could be seen in the distance as they slipped in through the early-morning mist to pick up the many infantry companies scattered in the area. Just before the twelve Hueys flew in to pick up our entire company, we learned that our destination was Vinh Loc Island, where Cocoa Beach was located. We were headed for the southernmost tip, some twenty miles away from the peaceful little naval fuel dump. We were told that no other American troops had been there before, and that it was being used by the North Vietnamese and VC as a rest and restaging area.

As we scrambled aboard the choppers, the thought came to me that this heliborne assault would be somewhat different: I would not be bearing the responsibility of a squad of soldiers, but was flying in with a chopper full of medics, RTOs, and a radio repair specialist. Our job would be to move in behind the advancing platoons and bring up rear security. It was a relief not to have the responsibility of eight or nine men on my shoulders, but I couldn't help but feel I had let down my squad by taking on my new responsibilities. I also knew I would miss the rush I had known dozens of times before as I raced from the Hueys with my buddies to engage the enemy.

Gaining altitude, our Hueys formed a tight formation and headed southeast into the beautiful orange sunrise. I gave the thumbs-up signal to one of my friends sitting in the doorway of the Huey flying beside us. Our ride was long and cold as the crisp morning air rushed through the choppers. The sight of the sun rising over the Gulf of Tonkin reminded me that even a war-ravaged country could steal an occasional moment of beauty and serenity.

Flying closer to the southern tip of Vinh Loc, we could pinpoint our destination by the plumes of dust and smoke belching skyward from the crashing of giant naval shells and supporting field artillery pieces. This operation was a joint effort of both Army and Navy. Several ships, which lay over the horizon, pounded the sleepy hamlets to soften our landing; dozens of Hueys and Chinooks flew in simultaneously like swarming bees. The magnitude of this unfolding operation frightened us —this would be a hard and brutal assault.

As the choppers descended toward a large sand flat, we scrambled out of the doorways and stood on the skids in order to have that precious one- or two-second advantage when the Hueys touched down. In the midst of the deafening roar of the engines and the blinding sand, we raced from the birds and fell flat on our bellies waiting for the choppers to leave and the whirling sandstorm to subside. We had expected the worst, but were puzzled at the ghostly silence that fell over us when the Hueys flew away. "What was going on? Where was the enemy?" These were the questions being asked as we picked ourselves up and formed into tactical elements. Alpha's three platoons moved out to cover various hamlets and tree lines, and the headquarters group spread out and fell in behind them.

"Mac" MacDonald, our radio repair specialist, and I had moved out to the right flank and were working our way through a small cluster of hootches when he pointed to a woman lying motionless near the mouth of a bunker. Less than ten feet away from her was a large, unexploded artillery shell that had landed nearby and lay silently like a ticking time bomb. The woman appeared dead, but Mac and I hesitated to approach her because of the dud artillery shell. After calling Doc Brailey, we walked over to the young woman and turned her over. It was one of the most horrifying sights I had ever seen. She had been hit in the stomach and chest by a large piece of artillery shrapnel, which had split her almost in half. I could have accepted this as just another war casualty, but this time it was different. She was pregnant, and the legs and feet of the fetus protruded from her ruptured belly.

Emotions raced through me—I didn't know whether to cry, vomit, or just turn and run away from that godforsaken place. The three of us were numbed by the sight, and we stood silently over her until Mac took off his rucksack and removed his poncho to cover her. For reasons that only a line doggie could understand, I suddenly found myself not caring at all about my personal safety. I walked over to the dud artillery shell, cradled it in my arms, and carried it nearly fifty yards away from the dead Vietnamese woman before putting it down. I don't know what possessed me to pick up the dangerous shell; I'd never done anything like that before. It was a foolish act, but I think I needed to show that my emotions weren't a casualty of this war, that the loss of a human life still meant something.

Working our way through the village, we rounded up the frightened civilians and moved them to a central collection point for interrogation. Van Long moved among them, trying to calm them. We could tell that they were extremely tense about our presence. Van Long jabbered excitedly to one old gentleman, obviously one of the village leaders. The old, weathered Vietnamese man wrung his hands and shuffled from foot to foot as he told Van his story. His wailing and moaning added to his tale of horror.

Van translated for us. The VC and NVA had been uneasy about the nonsupportive attitude of the local civilians and in order to convince them to provide support, the communist soldiers had marched the entire village population to a large field and picked the oldest man and the youngest baby from their midst. The old man was told to hold the baby in his arms and walk away from the crowd. When the old man reached a certain point, several enemy soldiers raised their rifles and mowed them down. An ultimatum was then given: if the village did not give its full support to the communist movement, the same thing would happen each day until they were satisfied that the villagers were not pro-American.

This was the straw that broke the camel's back, and our anger and hatred for the communist troops swelled beyond control. Such a horrible deed instilled in me the belief that communism should be forever confronted no matter what the costs, and I promised myself I would kill the next enemy soldier I laid eyes on.

We continued to gather up the civilians and comfort them with food and medical attention; after a brief interrogation, they were released to go back to their hootches. Many of them returned, bringing others with them, after they realized we were there not just to drive out the Viet Cong and North Vietnamese, but also to bring goodwill and peace to their remote little corner of the world. We spent the next two days wandering about the beautiful coastal villages of Vinh Loc without seeing so much as a trace of the enemy. We couldn't understand how they had vanished into thin air. The civilians confirmed that they had been there in numbers, and they had no idea where they had disappeared to since our assault had begun. One of our sister elements from the 502nd had made slight contact and killed or captured a dozen of the enemy. But they were supposed to be here by the scores—where were they?

We continued to search the quiet little hamlets nestled among the palm trees. Moving among the hootches, I stopped momentarily to light a cigarette and take a drink from my canteen. Standing with one foot propped on a pile of concrete blocks, I noticed a plastic package buried beneath three or four of the broken blocks. Tossing aside the rubble, I extracted a neatly wrapped bundle of papers and documents written in Vietnamese. Not realizing the magnitude of my find, I turned them over to Lieutenant Melton, who summoned the CO and Van Long. Van's eyes grew large as he read through the papers and jabbered to himself. He informed us that we had found communist tax records, with the names of all the local Viet Cong. The package was rewrapped in its plastic cover and tagged for shipment to the brigade intelligence officers.

Less than an hour later, while rambling along a palm-shaded trail bordering a tremendously large rice paddy, one of the National Police frantically pointed toward the center of the paddy and shouted, "VC! VC!" We could detect nothing, but the platoon of NPs jabbered excitedly to themselves and raced over the grass-covered dikes toward where the Vietnamese soldier had pointed. We watched in amazement as the National Police gathered along a large dike, screaming and aiming their rifles at the lush green rice plants. In a matter of seconds, two water-logged enemy soldiers emerged from under the long stalks of rice, their hands raised in a gesture of surrender. By the time the NPs finished, they had gathered up seven of the wet, weary enemy soldiers. They told an unbelievable story of how our early-morning assault had caught them completely by surprise and their only alternative had been to race for cover in the three feet of leech-infested paddy water, pulling the long, tangled stalks of rice over their heads. They were in pitiful shape, for they had hidden in the paddies for more than two days without sleep or food, and their shriveled bodies were covered with long, green leeches and festering sores.

An order was issued for us to spread out and walk the crisscrossed network of rice dikes in search of more of the enemy soldiers, while two Hueys were brought in to hover low over the rice fields and blow the long, unripened plants into the water. By late afternoon, we had captured nearly a hundred of the enemy, and had discovered that many of the larger dikes had small caves dug into their banks, with the entrances just under the water's surface. We weren't about to venture into these underwater hideouts, so we cleared them of enemy soldiers by tossing in grenades and jumping back before the tops of the dikes erupted in geysers of mud and water.

Tray Efird tossed a grenade into one of the underwater caves, and two half-naked VC stumbled from it after the grenade blew off its top. Stunned and wounded from the concussion, they floundered around in the muddy water, struggling to pull a third companion from their hiding place. Blood trickled from their nostrils and ears by the time they ceased their efforts to retrieve their dead friend, who floated facedown in the bubbling muck and slime. I raced over to assist Tray, who was dancing excitedly on top of the dike, pointing his rifle at the two enemy soldiers and shouting, *"Chieu hoi! Chieu hoi!"* They had absolutely no fight left in them, and spent their remaining energy by climbing from the muddy water and collapsing on the grassy dike. As Tray and I stood over them, I remembered the promise I had made to myself, and I raised my rifle muzzle to the head of one of the wounded soldiers. Tray said nothing as he realized what I was about to do. A sudden feeling of pride and self-respect rushed over me, and I found myself unable to lower my standards to the same level as those of the communists. An inner voice was screaming, "Shoot! Shoot!" yet another was pleading, "No!" In my anguish and frustration I turned and fired a round into the dead VC floating in the paddy. I have often felt shame over shooting the dead soldier, but it was the only way I could vent the anger and hatred that gnawed at my insides.

As evening approached, Alpha Company moved to the large sand dunes that paralleled the beach. Trip flares were placed over the vast network of paddy dikes so we could detect any of the remaining enemy trying to slip from the rice fields under cover of darkness. A new scout dog and handler were flown in just before dusk. The young Spec 4 told us he had just arrived in Vietnam with his dog; this was their first operation. Sensing his nervousness, and knowing no one wanted to bed down near the unfamiliar German shepherd, the CO instructed the dog handler to set up a position near the company CP.

As the evening wore on, an old woman triggered one of the nearby trip flares, and a couple of warning shots were fired to scare her back to her hootch. None of the vets of Alpha Company were concerned about the old woman, but we did not know that the incident had frightened our inexperienced dog handler into thinking we were under attack.

I had stretched out on the warm sand to get a couple of hours sleep before my turn at pulling radio guard when a sudden burst of automatic-rifle fire erased the peaceful murmur of the nearby waves. The shots were very close, and I grabbed my rifle and rolled myself into a clump of thorny bushes. When the firing stopped, I searched for signs of trouble. In less than a minute, someone was shouting, "Medic!" Doc Brailey was sleeping less than ten feet from me, and he asked me to go with him in case he needed help. We reached the 1st Platoon about the same time as the CO and another medic, and we were told that Lieutenant Smith's position had been fired on.

When we reached his position, we found the lieutenant writhing on the ground with a bullet hole through his left knee. A young Pfc from Florida, nicknamed "Gator," was lying still in the sand with a bullet through his chest. I held a red-lensed flashlight as Doc Brailey and another medic went to work over the limp body of Gator. We could tell he was still alive by the frothy blood that bubbled from his chest wound every time he took a breath. Remarkably, he came to and tried to sit up, pulling the IV needle from his arm. The spunky little private asked, "How bad am I hit?"

Making litters out of ponchos, we carried the two wounded soldiers to the beach to wait for a dust-off. As I kneeled beside them for what seemed an eternity, Gator started getting scared and talking irrationally about how he was going to die. This was a sure sign he was going into shock. The calm, reassuring voice of Doc Brailey was not doing the job of getting Gator's mind off his sucking chest wound. As the minutes slipped by, his condition worsened; I knew something had to be done immediately or we would lose him. I got down on my hands and knees and put my face close to his as he continued to mumble about dying. I shocked Gator, along with the highly religious Doc Brailey, when I began to insult him, and his family, with a blast of vulgar adjectives. Gator lay still for a moment, so I let him have it again with even more emphasis on the vulgarity. He said something about kicking my butt, so I cursed him again and challenged him to get up and try if he thought he was big enough. He grabbed my shirt and cursed back at me, and we let fly at each other with every profanity we could think of. I felt like an idiot kneeling over my wounded buddy and insulting him, but Doc Brailey and the other medics didn't say a word. They realized what I was doing, and most important of all, that what I was doing was working.

As a medevac homed in on our strobe light, we guided him into the edge of the surf so that dry sand would not be blown over our wounded. Gator's condition had improved greatly by the time we loaded him aboard the dust-off, and he managed to give us a thumbs-up sign as we lifted him gently to the outstretched hands of the chopper medics. We heard later that he had made it and was recovering in an army hospital in Louisiana. I never laid eyes on him again after the medevac chopper flew off down the dark beach, and I've often wondered if he ever realized that my sole purpose for cursing him was to save his life.

When we returned to the perimeter, we learned that the dog handler had been the one who fired into Lieutenant Smith's position. He had seen movement in the dark shadows to his front and figured it was enemy soldiers. No one had thought to inform him that he was in the middle of the perimeter—not on its outer edge.

The following day found us again searching the wide rice paddies for more of the evasive enemy soldiers, and our efforts turned up dozens more, who gladly surrendered so they could climb from their miserable hiding places. A few of us were walking the high ground of the sand dunes near a remote corner of a large paddy when a National Police soldier shouted, "VC!" and pointed to a black head of hair that momentarily glistened in the bright sun. The enemy soldier was approximately seventy or eighty yards from us, making his way toward a nearby tree line to escape our small patrol of GIs and NPs. As his head disappeared below the tall rice plants, Tray and I decided we would try to capture him instead of firing blindly at where he had last been. I shouted for Tray to bring his rifle, and I shed the weight of my rucksack, rifle, and helmet so I could try to run down the enemy soldier as he crawled through three feet of water and rice plants. Tray stayed on my heels as we raced across the dikes; if the enemy soldier stood up with a weapon in his hand, I was going to dive into the paddy and let Tray shoot him. The Viet Cong disappeared, and we stopped and waited for a telltale rustle of the thick, matted rice plants that totally concealed him. Spotting him again, the chase was on. It didn't take long to cover the few remaining yards between us. Going as far as possible on the dike, I plunged into the warm, dirty paddy water and began wading through the plants. Tray stood on the dike, his rifle trained toward the enemy soldier. My heart raced with excitement as I spotted him less than ten feet away. When I reached out to grab him, he jumped up and popped me on the chin with a tightly clenched fist. I was so surprised that I stumbled backward and fell into the water, the rice plants holding fast to my churning legs. The enemy soldier realized his mistake when Tray shouted at him and pointed the rifle at his chest. Seeing that he had no weapon, I jumped to my feet and tackled him. Tray cheered me on from the sidelines. I felt like drowning the small enemy soldier, but chose instead to vent my anger by giving him a dose of his own medicine. We splashed around in the dirty water while I gave him a good thrashing. I dragged him to the dike, where we both collapsed in exhaustion. I then bound my prisoner's hands with his belt and marched him nearly a mile back to where our CO had set up a command post for collecting the POWs.

By the time we reached the CP, my emotions and anger had calmed down somewhat. I guided the prisoner over to a group of his comrades, lit up a cigarette, and stuck it between his swollen lips. I couldn't help but have respect for the feisty little soldier, but at the same time, I hated everything he stood for.

The National Police decided they would take it upon themselves to interrogate the small group of Viet Cong and North Vietnamese we had captured. Those of us near the CP watched curiously as the South Vietnamese took a few of the enemy soldiers and tied their hands and feet. The pitifully frightened POWs were then carried down to the beach, where there were bamboo poles driven into the sand for drying and untangling fishnets. The NPs lifted the enemy with their feet skyward, draping the ropes over the top of the bamboo pilings. As the POWs hung with their heads and shoulders touching the sand, the NPs took long, limber bamboo poles and beat the soles of their feet until they bled. It didn't take long before they had every one of the POWs answering their questions. The National Police then cut them down and dragged them back to the palm-shaded dunes.

Bud and his squad soon came in with five more prisoners and several captured weapons slung over their shoulders. Bud knew I had been looking for a nonautomatic weapon that I could register and take home as a souvenir. He had two old rifles in his hands and said, "Take your pick." I reached for a World War II K-44 Russian carbine that looked as though it hadn't been cleaned since the first day it was issued. I was amazed at what poor condition we were finding our enemy's weapons to be in. Thanking Bud, I tagged the old bolt-action rifle and placed it in a growing pile of weapons to be sent back to LZ Sally.

In three more days, our operation ended. We gathered our forces for extraction from that lovely island paradise, where we had pulled off one of the most classic operations of the entire Vietnam War. Our final tally was 154 enemy killed, 370 enemy captured, and 56 enemy *Chieu hois* (enemy soldiers who voluntarily surrendered their arms), along with tons of captured weapons and supplies. Our only losses were two killed and nine wounded. For once, we had held the upper hand over our enemy and had dealt him a severe blow in an area he had controlled for a long time.

As we gathered in small chopper loads to be lifted out, we were ecstatic to hear we would not be going back to Eight-Klick Ville. This was the news we had long been waiting on—it didn't matter where we were going as long as it wasn't back to that hellhole we had grown to despise.

Our sortie of Hueys flew away from Vinh Loc, turned, and headed north toward a large coastal area dotted with small, inhabited villages. We learned that Alpha Company was to move in and build a new star-shaped fire base called "Sandy." As we landed, it became obvious that the fire base was not named for some girl back home, but for the snow-white, powdery sand that nearly blinded us as it reflected the sun's rays. Not only was it uncomfortable to our eyes, but it also reflected the ultraviolet rays and burned our skin.

During the building of the new base, a bulldozer, slung in by a flying crane, covered up a small cluster of graves while digging a garbage sump. A few of the villagers began the laborious task of removing the tons of sand that had been spread over the graves. They dug for nearly two days to exhume the bodies from the covered graves and rebury their loved ones in another location. Late in the second day of their digging, Doc Brailey and I walked over to see how they were doing. A frail, old man hobbled over to us holding something wrapped in a dirty rag. He motioned to the deep hole he had helped dig, talking to us as though we understood every word. Then he unwrapped the object in his hands, showing us a sand-covered skull complete with black (betel nut-stained) teeth. Doc and I were caught completely off guard, and we stuttered and stammered at the old gentleman as he whimpered over the skull and flicked sand from it with his thin, crooked fingers.

We stayed at Sandy for several days while two of our platoons worked on the perimeter bunkers, and a third pulled search-and-clear patrols in the nearby villages. News reached us of a tragic event that happened to Charlie Company, which instilled in our minds a doubtful feeling about the ARVNs and National Police who had worked with us in the recent past. A squad from Charlie Company had been assigned to guard a bridge with another squad of South Vietnamese PF soldiers. One night as the GIs at the bridge slept beside the South Vietnamese popular forces, the PFs gunned them down, along with the handful of unsuspecting paratroopers who were pulling guard. The PF soldiers were never seen again, and the mystery of why this happened was never solved.

Only the well-trained ARVN soldiers were sent out to work with us after that. No one felt safe around the poorly trained, ill-equipped South Vietnamese popular forces. They were the lowest echelon of Vietnamese fighting troops, considered more or less the "home guard." They hung around villages by day and then went home when darkness fell and the VC came out to prowl.

CHAPTER SEVEN

GOING HOME

I'll never forget the day I was taken off the "line." I had been waiting on that joyous day for almost eleven months, and when it finally came, it was as though I had been given a new lease on life. First Sergeant Soward approached me while Alpha Company was still at Sandy, and advised me that I was now one of the "privileged few": I had received three Purple Hearts and could leave the boonies, as long as a base-camp job was open. At this point, I would have accepted the lowly job of ol' Willie the shit burner, for as the twelve-month tour of a line doggie started "gettin' short," his nerves began to play tricks on him—he was constantly worried about making it through the last four or five weeks of combat.

"Top" Soward asked if I would rather stay in the fields or remain at fire base Sandy and control the shuttling of food and supplies between the fire base and the infantry companies it supported. Of course, I accepted the latter. I was then introduced to another E-5 buck sergeant who would be working with me. My responsibilities would be to control the supplies and food on the PSP (perforated steel planking) chopper pad lying just outside the perimeter. I had two Pfc's working with me, and we would see to it that the log ships were packed with the proper loads and sent on their way to the waiting companies of infantrymen.

The other E-5, Tim Rochell, stayed within the perimeter and controlled the choppers by radio, coordinating their flights between Sandy and each company in our battalion. Call it fate or simply bad chemistry, but for some reason, Sergeant Rochell and I just didn't get along. One problem I had with him was the fact that he had no sympathy for line doggies, since his entire eleven months in Nam had been served from a supply tent—he had never humped the boonies or slept in the mud. It was good for both of us that our contact consisted mainly of radio conversation from his tent and my chopper pad. We did come to blows one evening after he made a sarcastic remark about my buddies in Alpha Company.

I worked as supply coordinator at Sandy for the next two-and-a-half weeks and helped shuttle tons of supplies, food, ammo, and fresh water out to the troops. It was a good feeling to be out of the boonies. The closest I came to combat during my short stay at Sandy occurred one night when the VC dropped a few mortar rounds inside our perimeter. No one was hurt by the hastily fired shells, but the jagged shrapnel managed to puncture a large fuel bladder full of gasoline, which quickly disappeared into the snow-white sand.

Just before leaving Sandy, I heard some news of my old outfit: "ol' 3-5" had been relieved of his duties as platoon sergeant. Alpha Company had been working the populated villages around Highway One, and Major Canton, our battalion XO, had caught him in a local brothel with several cans of beer under his belt. He was being transferred out of the battalion and sent down south to work in one of the base camps near Bien Hoa. In some ways, I felt sorry for him, but his leaving was the best thing that could have happened to Alpha Company—especially to the 3rd Platoon. Bud had been made platoon sergeant, which greatly pleased me, but I knew this spoiled his chances of being pulled from the field for some safer job within the confines of a base camp. Bud was now destined to spend the rest of his tour humping the paddies, helping to guide our old platoon through the VC-infested villages and hamlets. It was fitting that he had taken over the duties of Eddie Hands, whom he had greatly admired.

After almost three weeks of working at Sandy, I left the small, star-shaped fire base and returned to LZ Sally to prepare to go on R & R. I was excited about the week I would spend in Sydney, Australia, and spent nearly half a day packing my meager belongings in an AWOL bag —a line doggie could usually carry everything he owned in one hand.

My journey to Australia would start from Ton Son Nhut Air Base, so I would first have to fly south and proceed through Bien Hoa, the administrative replacement center for the entire 101st Airborne Division. Arriving at Bien Hoa late in the afternoon, I spent that night at the huge complex before catching a commercial airliner the next day. It was at Bien Hoa that I happened to run into an old MP buddy from Fort Bragg. Steve Standridge and I had been friends since our paratrooper training and had not seen each other since we parted ways nearly a year-and-a-half earlier. He was on his way home to Stockton, California, with less than three days left in Vietnam. We hitched a ride to the NCO club and spent the next few hours swapping tales about our experiences and drowning the memories of our lost friends with can after can of mind-numbing beer. Steve had spent most of his tour humping the boonies of Nam in a specialized reconnaissance group called a "Tiger Team," so he had developed an acute case of the nervous jitters just as I had. As we reminisced in the dimly lit, smoke-filled club, a young Vietnamese waitress dumped a tray full of empty beer cans into a large steel drum. Steve and I, wrapped up in our conversation and not expecting the sudden crash, suddenly found ourselves flat on the dirty floor, sprawled in puddles of spilled beer, trying not to show our embarrassment. Those in the club who had never spent time in the boonies laughed at us, but those who had humped the jungles and paddies sat quietly; they understood what it was like to jump like a frightened deer at the slightest noise.

After a delightful, sun-filled week in Sydney, I returned to LZ Sally with less than three weeks before my year-long tour would end. I learned that my job at fire base Sandy had been filled; I was somewhat glad of that because I had had my fill of living at the hot, little camp. I considered going back to the boonies, but found out that battalion needed an E-5 to be in charge of a supply truck that made daily runs to remote guard posts such as bridges, water towers, railroad trestles, and even a small marine camp. I asked for the job and soon found out why no one else had volunteered. Since the supply truck made such a long journey, it had to leave base camp before all of the roads had been cleared of land mines. Also, several areas along the route were perfect for being ambushed or fired on by a VC sniper.

The same driver picked me up each morning at Alpha's hootch, and from there we proceeded to make several stops to load water, hot food, mail, and ammunition for the soldiers who manned the positions along our route. The driver was a young, pudgy kid with short, blonde hair and a fat face that had never been shaved. His face was full of pimples and blemishes. He was friendly, though, and was always smiling, allowing juice from the chew of tobacco in his jaw to ooze out and stain the corners of his mouth. He was also very nervous about being ambushed, and drove the two-and-a-half-ton truck like an Indianapolis race car. His claim to fame was the two bullet holes in the hood of his truck from a sniper's rifle.

Our daily trip over the hot, dusty roads was long and boring, often ending with a mad rush to make it back to LZ Sally before darkness caught us bouncing over the thousands of potholes that riddled the Vietnamese highway system. The only enjoyable part of our journey from one outpost to another came toward the end of the day, when we stopped at a pumping station and water tower perched precariously on the banks of the Perfume River near Hue. Since it was our last stop, we were able to feed the leftover food from the mermite cans to the dozens of children who lived on the riverside in bamboo hootches. They had learned to come running at the sound of our truck and would stand patiently while we fed the GIs, knowing they would soon partake of the steaming leftovers we would dish out to them on paper plates. The mere presence of these innocent children brightened our day and helped erase thoughts of the constant death and suffering that raged around us.

With each passing hour, I grew more anxious about the approaching day marking my return to CONUS (Continental United States). My spirits were flying high, and the only thing that bothered me at this point was the increasing harassment that came with working in a base camp. Combat duty in Vietnam had been comparatively free of the nitpicking rules and regulations we had been used to back in the States, but now the base camps were becoming just like garrison duty at any military fort. Young, rank-hungry officers tried to outdo each other with nonsensical details and foolish regulations. Long before we left Fort Campbell, we had been issued cloth "jungle hats," which were worn in base camps and also by line doggies on night ambush patrols. They were light and comfortable and were willingly substituted for the heavy steel pots that were mandatory in the fields. One of those hats would almost cost me an Article 15 and a demotion from sergeant to corporal.

An order had been recently issued that no jungle hats would be worn out of base camp, but on our daily trips to deliver supplies and food, my young driver ignored this directive. He tossed his helmet on the seat and replaced it with his "flop hat," because the constant bouncing over potholes slammed our helmets against our heads like sledgehammers.

On one trip we were observed by Major Canton as his jeep raced past us in downtown Hue. I had not even noticed our battalion XO, for the streets were busy with smoke-belching Lambrettas and scores of military vehicles. He wrote down our truck number and issued an order for the ranking NCO in charge of the truck to be fined and demoted because the driver was not wearing a helmet.

When we returned to LZ Sally late in the afternoon, First Sergeant Soward was waiting on our truck and broke the news that I was in trouble. I couldn't believe a minor incident such as that was going to cost me my stripes, but there it was all typed out and ready for my signature—"Article 15." "Top" Soward handed it to me and calmly stated, "Read it and sign it." I did so and handed it back to him, speechless with anger. "Top" folded the paper, sealed it in an envelope, and as he turned to walk away he gave me a wink and said quietly, "You have just been given an Article 15. Now if you keep your mouth shut and if no one asks any questions, this envelope will soon find its way into a trash can." In my anger and frustration, it was hard for me to find the words to express my appreciation, but I'm sure the smile on my face assured him that I was grateful for his understanding. If he hadn't taken the matter into his own hands, I would have been victimized by one of the foolish rules that plagued us all.

My tour in Vietnam was quickly coming to an end. I would soon be going home for a thirty-day leave and then a final six-month tour of duty at some installation in the States. I was hoping to be assigned to Fort Bragg, North Carolina, because it was close to home, and I was familiar with the giant army fort, having spent nearly a year there before reporting to Fort Campbell. My chances of assignment were good, because most of the DEROS-ing troopers from the 101st were being sent back to finish their hitches in the 82nd Airborne Division.

Our original company members were coming in from the fields to start the long process of preparing to leave Vietnam; having come from Fort Campbell as a complete company, those who had survived the past year of combat would be leaving on the same date. As that date drew nearer, our small company hootch bulged with young men who all had the same excuse to celebrate and throw a beer party every night. The atmosphere around LZ Sally was almost festive as literally hundreds of troopers from the 2nd Brigade prepared to take the "freedom bird" home. It was hard to find chores for all of the idle hands, and I'm sure the NCOs and officers at Sally would be glad to see us go so things would return to normal and they could get back to running the war.

Our nights were occupied by crowding into the dimly lit hootches and either playing poker with abnormally high stakes or reminiscing over a cooler of beer, trying to outdo each other with tales of our experiences during the last twelve months. Horseplay was inevitable in this boisterous group, and one particular incident nearly sent Ric Ricart to the hospital. He and Tom Cashion, who were the best of friends, got a little carried away with a foolish game of tussle. They playfully pulled knives on each other, taking dangerous swipes to see how close they could come with the razor-sharp blades without actually drawing blood. Neither had the intention of hurting the other, but I could see their game was getting out of hand. "Cash" took a roundhouse swing at Ric and slit the front of his loosely hanging fatigue shirt. I could tell by the expression on Ric's face that he had been cut. They stared at each other in disbelief, and Ric slowly lifted his shirt to expose a twelve-inch slice running horizontally just above his naval. A thick layer of fat bulged from the opening and blood slowly trickled down his belly into the top of his pants. They both turned a ghostly shade of white and immediately began to think up cover stories about how the accident occurred. There was no reason to cause trouble at that point. I made up my mind to go along with whatever story they came up with so they would not be fined and possibly detained from their flight home.

Helping Ric to the aid station, we found out that his injury was not as serious as we had first thought; he was sewn up and wrapped in sterile bandages. When the doctors asked questions about how Ric had ripped open his stomach, he calmly lied and said he had fallen into a roll of concertina wire. After he was treated, we returned to Alpha's hootch and the accident was soon forgotten.

On the morning of our departure, we were filled with excitement and joy, but felt somewhat melancholy about saying good-bye to the many friends we were leaving behind. A small formation was held in front of our hootch, and we were informed that we would be flown to the Hue-Phu Bai airport on a Chinook. We were to be at the helipad at 1100 for our final flight out of LZ Sally. Termination papers and reassignment orders were distributed. "Going home" was finally becoming a reality.

Long before our departure time, most of us had gathered at the PSP chopper pad, anxiously awaiting the first leg of our "freedom flight." Bud and I were leaving together. As we stood around with a small group of our close friends, he nudged me with his elbow and pointed to a lone figure making its way around the camp ammo dump and heading in our direction. It was Van Long, and we soon found out that he had hitchhiked to LZ Sally after getting permission to leave the company and come say good-bye.

As he made his way toward us, I knew those final few minutes with him would not be easy. I found myself wishing our chopper would come and take us away. Van walked up to Bud and me and wrapped his arms around us as a single tear found its way down each side of his face. The three of us slowly walked away from the crowd; Bud and I tried to choke back our emotions, but failed when Van said, "I come to say good-bye to Sholly and Dykes." I could tell Bud was hurting inside as much as I was, for we both knew we would never see our devoted little friend again. We stood there and awkwardly conversed for several minutes until our Chinook flew in and settled to the pad. As the tailgate lowered, Bud and I turned to Van and once again embraced him in a gesture of true friendship. I'll always remember the expression on his face—it was the worried look of a lost child. I wondered if anyone in Alpha Company would look after him the way Bud and I had. When the big transport chopper strained its engines and lifted from the pad, we turned our heads to catch one last glimpse of Van. He never saw us smile as he stood alone in the whirling dust and waved while our chopper groaned skyward and turned toward Hue.

We spent an uneventful night at the Hue-Phu Bai airport and grew more impatient as our time of departure drew closer. The next day we were led out to the apron of the runway and were told to sit beneath the wings of a C-130 Hercules to escape the blistering heat of the sun while we waited on the pilots. As we sat in the hot shade, someone pointed to a section near one of the engines where the word "Crack" had been written with a felt-tip marker. An arrow was drawn to an "X" obviously marking a weak place in the wing. Everyone wondered about the warning, but we all laughed and assured ourselves that anyone who had gotten this far through his tour in "The Nam" would certainly not be intimidated by a mere crack in an airplane wing.

Our flight south on the groaning transport craft was long and boring —all we had to do for nearly three hours was sit on the webbed seats and stare at each other. Talking was almost impossible over the drone of the engines, so those of us who couldn't sleep simply sat alone with our thoughts and daydreamed about how it would be when we finally got home.

We arrived at the huge replacement center at Bien Hoa and spent the rest of the afternoon turning in our rifles and making final clearances on the volumes of paperwork that were being processed on every paratrooper. With absolutely nothing to do, most of us made our way to the NCO and EM clubs and whiled away the afternoon hours over countless cans of beer.

The next morning found our small group waiting patiently in a chow line that stretched for nearly a hundred yards. Just as many new replacements filled the chow line as did seasoned veterans, and I can vividly recall how easy it was to distinguish between the two. The vets wore fatigues, almost turned gray from sweat and the bleaching sun, and boots, once shiny black, now scuffed brown. The vets' faces were tan, and wrinkles had sprouted around their eyes from squinting in the bright Vietnam sun; cigarettes hung from their lips in a "don't give a damn" fashion. The cherries seemed nervous and stood out in the crowd with their new boots, fatigues, and untanned faces. Most of them stood quietly, straining their ears to pick up bits of the vets' conversations.

Slowly working our way toward the steaming aroma of eggs, sausage, pancakes, coffee, and other breakfast foods, Bud and I talked casually with several of our friends about our reassignment orders. I had received orders for the 82nd Airborne Division at Fort Bragg, North Carolina, and someone commented about how lucky I was to be assigned to a fort so close to my home. A young cherry standing quietly in front of us turned and asked, "Are you from North Carolina?" In a matter of seconds, we found out we were both from the same hometown and had gone to the same high school. I invited him to sit with us during breakfast so we could talk more about the people and places both of us were missing so much. Before we parted, he confided that he was scared to death, and he asked me what it was like to pull a year's hitch in an infantry company. I tried to ease his mind a bit, but I could tell he was going to have a hard time of it, since he had been drafted and didn't want to fight in such an unpopular war. I never saw him again after those brief moments we shared together, but I found out he had lost his life about a month later in the highly publicized battle of Hamburger Hill.

Later that day we were bused to Ton Son Nhut, where we were

crammed into barracks and told we would receive our flight information later that evening. The atmosphere had almost turned into that of a carnival, as hundreds of GIs waited to hear their names called on a flight manifest. Before the day ended, we were ordered to a formation and told to bring everything we owned. Forming up with our belongings at our feet, we were then instructed to dump our duffle bags out on the ground while a team of officers went through everything, searching for drugs, weapons, explosives, and other contraband. To me, it seemed degrading to have to go through that, but I soon understood why it was necessary when I saw the pile of confiscated illegal merchandise that was destined to be smuggled out of Vietnam.

Early the next morning, we were awakened by the shrill cry of a whistle. A sergeant came through each of the Quonset huts, barking out orders—we were to be dressed, through with breakfast, and in formation by 0700. No one objected, since this was "The Big Day," but we couldn't understand the hurry since our flights didn't leave until midafternoon.

Making that first formation was no problem for most of us, but a few had to put forth their maximum effort just to stand up straight. They were suffering immensely from the gallons of beer they had consumed the night before. It appeared as though we would have to put up with the usual army harassment right up until the last minute, since we were made to stand in formation for nearly two hours before a team of sergeants and lieutenants came and once again ordered us to empty our duffle bags. No one could believe we were having another shakedown less than twelve hours after the first one, but this second invasion of privacy turned up another full box of contraband.

Stuffing our belongings back into the duffle bags, we then boarded the same type of whistling army buses that had picked us up at the air base exactly one year earlier. The sides of the olive-drab buses were draped with dusty banners that read "Screaming Eagles—Going Home." I felt like a prisoner as I peered out through the heavy wire mesh welded over the windows to prevent grenades from being tossed inside as the buses made their way through the ghettos surrounding the air base.

When we reached the dusty, open-air terminal building, we were ordered inside. A lieutenant shouted over a bullhorn once again, calling our names from the flight manifest. We were instructed to answer when our names were called. It turned into a comedy routine as the jubilant soldiers acknowledged their names with everything from "Hallelujah" and "Airborne" to "California Bound" and "Hot Damn."

Small groups of friends stood around the busy terminal and downed soft drinks from the snack bar, anxiously smoking one cigarette after another. A few of us found empty seats and decided to rest while waiting on our freedom bird. As I was sitting and pondering over the last 365 days of my life, a frail, old mamasan worked her way through the rows of broken-down metal chairs, sweeping up thousands of cigarette butts. I remember thinking that my last day in Vietnam was turning out to be very much like the first—both had started with a ride on a whistling bus and ended with an old Vietnamese woman with a smile full of "black pearl" teeth, sweeping around my feet with a worn-out broom.

Each time a bomb-ladened jet fighter growled its engines, we would throw a quick glance toward the runway to see if the noise was coming from our long-awaited commercial craft. Finally, the most beautiful red and white TWA jet that any of us had ever seen, landed and seemed to shout at us to come climb aboard when the pilot threw the huge jet engines into reverse. A cheer rose from the crowd as we stood on the rickety chairs to try to get a better look at the taxiing jetliner.

Within minutes, we were led outside into the hot sun, where we stood quietly as a load of cherries filed from the plane. There were a few catcalls from our group, and I felt sure they had come from troops who had served their tour in a safe base-camp job. The line doggies, who had experienced the horrors of fighting in the boonies, watched silently, either out of respect or pity, for they knew what that fresh batch of replacements was about to be introduced to. I remembered a similar experience we had had at Wake Island, and I felt sorry for those young, green soldiers. I wondered how many of their numbers would make it home alive.

We were quickly loaded aboard the airliner while it was being refueled: the commercial jets had strict instructions to spend as little time as possible in Vietnam. As we roared down the runway, a joyous cheer rose from the GIs. We craned to peer out the windows and take one last look at that beautiful yet vicious country which had been the stage for an unforgettable chapter in our lives. From the air, Vietnam looked beautiful, with its lush green jungles and meandering rivers, but there was a distinct characteristic that marked it as the world's current battle-field—as far as one could see, the landscape was pocked with bomb craters. They looked like open sores that had festered and burst, allowing the earth's rich crust to spew forth and stand out against the dark-green growth.

Our homeward-bound flight stopped in Okinawa and Hawaii for refueling, continuing on to its final destination at Travis Air Force Base in California. It was a cold, rainy December afternoon when we landed at Travis, and we were elated when we touched down on the puddle-covered runway. For some foolish reason we thought there would be some kind of welcoming party, but those hopeful thoughts were squelched as our pilot taxied to the rear of a huge hangar and shut down the engines.

As we left the plane and headed toward a small concrete building adjacent to the hangar, I wondered where the brass bands were, and the crowds cheering and waving Old Glory, just as I had seen them do in the World War II movies. We splashed across the concrete apron and made our way through the cold rain. As we approached the cinder-block building, someone pointed to a canvas sign barely visible in the fading light. It had been hung between two windows and was supposed to have read "Welcome Home," but one end of the sign had come loose in the blustery weather and had fallen down, so the message read "Welcome Ho." One clever soldier from our tired group asked if Ho Chi Minh had been on our flight.

Once inside, we were led to a large, empty room with long yellow lines painted on the floor. After a short wait, our duffle bags were carted in to us; we were instructed to find our baggage, then line up with our toes on the yellow line and our belongings piled in front of us. This was the third shakedown in the last thirty-six hours, but most of us were too tired to be angry. We wanted to get on with processing, so with few words we dumped out our bags and another team of sergeants picked through them in search of war-zone contraband.

Next we were herded to a large, gymlike area with bleachers for us to sit on. A young officer came in and gave us a speech about the benefits of reenlisting; almost everyone laughed out loud at the mere thought of re-uping and possibly pulling another tour in Vietnam. Winter uniforms, airline tickets, and travel money were next on the agenda; before we had all of our chores completed, nearly four hours had passed since we stepped from the plane.

Chartered buses took us to the San Francisco International Airport, and from there we scattered to make the connections that would distribute us to all corners of the United States. We gathered for one last time to shake hands and say goodbye to the many friends and close buddies that we knew we would never see again. Quite a few GIs had finished their hitch in the Army and would not be reporting to Fort Bragg or other military posts.

I flew for what seemed like all night, finally reaching Atlanta, where I was scheduled to catch one more flight in the early morning to my final destination. My final flight took less than an hour, and a hard rain greeted my plane as we dropped through the clouds and landed at the Charlotte airport.

As I stepped from the plane, I stood in the early-morning rain and soaked up the emotional rush of finally being back home. A lump rose in my throat and my eyes misted over as I realized that through my personal determination and faith in God, I had made it through a full year of living in Hell. As I moved among the small crowds of sleepy early-morning travelers, I felt pride and personal accomplishment in the medals and battle ribbons decorating my chest. But suddenly I realized that no one really gave a damn—I was just another GI, in transit from point A to point B. I had the urge to shout, "Hey, look at me! I'm home! Don't you know what I've just been through?" Picking up my duffle bag and the old K-44 carbine I had brought back, I made my way out the front doors of the terminal to flag down a taxi.

The dispatcher whistled for the lead cab and asked where I was going. I detected a tone of disgust in his response when I told him I lived only a mile and a half from the airport. The driver didn't want to take me, since the fare would be small, but the dispatcher summoned me over to the cab; he would take me, but I would be charged a special rate for the short trip. I said, "Okay," and threw my belongings in the back seat.

The driver seemed mad as hell about having to take me such a short distance. As we pulled away from the terminal, I noticed he had not turned on his meter, so I questioned him about it.

"Hey, kid! I told you the fare would be a special rate, so I don't need to turn it on."

"But I thought you would still have to turn the meter on, sir."

"You damned GIs are all alike—always wanting something for nothing. Don't you realize I'm gonna have to go back to the airport and get at the end of the line when I could just as easily have had a $15 or $20 trip into Charlotte?"

"I'm sorry, sir, I don't want anything for free. I just want to get home and was thinking I would be charged the same rate as anyone else."

"Well, you agreed on the special rate, so that's final."

"Turn left, into this next driveway, sir. How much do I owe you?"

"That'll be eight bucks, kid."

"Here's ten dollars, sir. Keep the change. And by the way—Merry Christmas."

"Thanks kid. And, oh yeah—Merry Christmas to you, too."

I grabbed my duffle bag and rifle from the back seat and turned to see my parents rushing out the front door.

"Hey, Mama. Hey, Daddy. I'm home."